MORE ADVANCE PRAISE FOR
THE DHARMA of STAR WARS

❝ Bortolin [...] may be the ideal person to write about the Buddhist themes in Star Wars: he camped out for tickets to all of the movies—even the less than stellar ones—and possesses his own set of Jedi robes. [...] One of the book's greatest strengths is Bortolin's stubborn determination to find something redeeming about [Episodes I and II of the] Star Wars films, and he does actually recover enough of these nuggets to make fans take a second look at those overhyped flicks [...] With humor, strong examples and timeless wisdom, Bortolin offers a new way to think about a pop culture phenomenon.
Lead us to Yoda, he does. ❞
PUBLISHERS WEEKLY

❝ Star Wars fans will find Bortolin's pleasant humor and simple directness immensely enjoyable and thought provoking, while long-time spiritual practitioners will discover a new and profound avenue into self-transformation. ❞
ROBERT A. JOHNSON, AUTHOR OF "OWNING YOUR OWN SHADOW"

❝ Those movie lovers who haven't yet gotten their copy of the Star Wars trilogy on DVD may want to wait [until the release of The Dharma of Star Wars]—and achieve enlightenment at the same time. ❞
PW RELIGION BOOKLINE, FALL 2004

D0646193

THE DHARMA

STAR WARS

MATTHEW BORTOLIN

WISDOM PUBLICATIONS • BOSTON

Wisdom Publications, Inc.
199 Elm Street
Somerville MA 02144 USA
www.wisdompubs.org

Disclaimer: Neither this book nor its contents are endorsed or approved by or affiliated in any way with George Lucas or Lucasfilm Ltd. The opinions contained herein are those of the author only. Star Wars™ is the registered trademark of Lucasfilm Ltd. All rights reserved.

Nothing in this work, including the use of Star Wars characters, names, and scenarios is in any way intended to show association with or endorsement of any religion or philosophy.

Library of Congress Cataloging-in-Publication Data
Bortolin, Matthew.
  The dharma of Star wars / Matthew Bortolin.
     p. cm.
  Includes index.
  ISBN 0-86171-497-0 (pbk. : alk. paper)
  1. Religious life—Buddhism. 2. Star Wars films. I. Title.
  BQ5405.B67 2005
  294.3'367914375—dc22
                              2004029379

ISBN 0-86171-497-0
First Edition

09 08 07 06 05
5   4   3   2   1

Cover design by Patrick O'Brien. "Fanboy Monks" by Andrew Campbell. Interior design by DCummings, Inc. Set in Berkeley Book 11.5/16.25.

Printed in the United States of America.

MAY THE MERIT OF THIS WORK BENEFIT ALL BEINGS.

CONTENTS

PROLOGUE

I.

SNAPHISS! The red-bladed lightsaber arches through the air toward its target. At the last instant green-blade rises to meet it, locking the two in static tension. The battle of Jedi and Sith is rejoined.

This is no ordinary battle—but a fight between father and son with the fate of the galaxy, the balance of the Force, and so much more at stake—for as the two battle one another they also battle themselves. Luke Skywalker, the last living Jedi, has entered this fight in order to rescue his father from the abyss of evil, but the way to victory could mean losing himself to the dark side. Darth Vader, the man once known as Anakin Skywalker before he gave himself to the dark side, struggles to climb out of the darkness and return to the light of his former self.

The battle we see played out on the screen in breathtaking acrobatics and flashing green and red sabers is in reality the battle for the participants' very hearts and minds. Jedi and fallen-Jedi, both struggle to come to terms with themselves and the world, to confront the evil within them, and ultimately transcend it.

Yet the only way to win this momentous battle at its deepest level is to switch off the lightsaber—as Luke does an instant before he destroys his father—and truly break the hold of the dark side within each of us. The only way to real balance within our self and peace in the world is to face the dark side with openness and courage—and come to terms with the truth of reality as it is.

…but we're getting ahead of ourselves. Another part of our story begins two and a half millennia ago, on Earth, in a place called Kapilavastu.

II.

A LONG TIME AGO, IN A LAND FAR, FAR AWAY

there lived a man named Siddhartha Gautama. Siddhartha, the eldest son of a powerful king, dwelled in the very heart of luxury and self-indulgence. He was fed on lavish food and drink, and was lulled to sleep by the most melodious music. He was adorned with the finest jewelry and the softest silk. He was uncommonly handsome and graced with a regal bearing. When he came of age, he was blessed with a lovely wife who was both dignified and kind. Siddhartha had everything in life that we commonly believe should content a man—yet he could not find peace in his heart.

Siddhartha's comforts could not alleviate his fear of sickness, aging, and death. No pleasures could truly drive away the pain of sorrow, or the insatiable restlessness of life that we all suffer. For years he struggled with the dilemma of life's suffering, until one late night, at the age of twenty-nine, he left his palatial home—left even his beloved wife and young son—and forsook his claim to the throne of his father's kingdom. In this moment he went forth to free himself completely from all life's suffering.

Like a Padawan learning from great Jedi Masters, Siddhartha sought out the most respected spiritual teachers of his time and mastered the meditation techniques they taught. But he left each teacher because none could resolve for him the fundamental problems of life and death that plague all humans. And so he plunged ever forward in his quest, now into the forest and the life of an ascetic, a world-renouncer.

Siddhartha joined a group of men practicing intense austerities. They ate but a few grains of rice a day, savagely beat their own bodies, and practiced severe and painful forms of abstinence. Siddhartha was so resolute in his effort that he took his rigorous practice beyond any of his peers—even unto the point of nearly dying. And this taught him that asceticism would not be his salvation.

Siddhartha had lived the life of a decadent prince and a self-denying ascetic, and both paths had proved fruitless. And so he abandoned all the old traditions and began to blaze a new trail, a path that would later become known as the Middle Way. He turned his attention inward, observing his mind and the world of phenomena, no longer denying the world around him but no longer becoming intoxicated by it either. He began to live simply and joyfully.

He sat day and night in meditation, his understanding penetrating deeper and deeper until one night, while sitting at the foot of a strong tree, ignorance slipped from his mind like the haze of sleep from an awakening dreamer—and he awakened to truth. With this awakening came the transcendence of all suffering, freedom from all fear, and the direct and clear understanding of reality. From that day forward he was known as the Buddha—the Awakened One.

For the next forty-five years the Buddha shared his insights with the people of northeast India, and from there they have spread through the centuries and throughout the world. His teachings, known as the Dharma, detailed the way to be free from the shackles of birth and death, fear, anxiety, anger, jealousy, insecurity and all the other manifestations of suffering. This freedom, he taught, is attained through the cultivation of understanding and compassion. The Dharma shows us how to transform ignorance into wisdom, and greed and anger into compassion, so we may better love ourselves, our family, and all the world.

III.

THE STAR WARS SAGA is a story of human beings and other creatures grappling with issues of freedom, hate, love, power, and suffering. It is an exploration of the human condition writ large across a tale of galactic war, despair and hope, good and evil, and the struggle for peace. Star Wars is not a Buddhist epic. And yet because the Star Wars saga addresses so much of what it means to be human it can appropriately be applied to the Buddha's teachings, and the Buddha's teachings can effectively be used to illuminate our understanding of the characters and themes in Star Wars. The Dharma of Star Wars is an exploration of the deepest universal themes in the Star Wars saga, using Buddhist teachings to investigate them; simultaneously, it is also an introduction to the teachings of the Buddha, using Star Wars as a doorway through which to examine them.

When we look carefully at Anakin Skywalker, for instance, we can see that he was dissatisfied with life much like the Buddha was before he awakened. Siddhartha found no solace in the luxuries of his life as a prince; Anakin was unfulfilled by his existence on Tatooine and dreamed of becoming a great Jedi. Both fled the familiar, the easy, the known, in search of something more. Their paths led in different directions, but both demonstrate what it is to be human, how our ignorance and attachments lead to suffering, and how compassion and wisdom lead to freedom.

The heart of the Buddha's Way is the teaching of the Four Noble Truths. The first three truths proclaim: suffering exists; suffering has a cause; suffering can cease. The fourth truth outlines the Path leading to the cessation of suffering. Although the Buddha spoke of his insights as "truths," it is up to us to discover their validity—just as each Jedi must for himself experience and understand the Force. This means the Dharma is in no way dogmatic and should not be accepted solely on blind faith.

The Buddha traveled the Middle Way repeatedly, blazing a trail for us to walk, to reflect upon, and to realize in our own way. Personal observation is essential. We must observe our mind, our thoughts, the world around us, and in this way we come to truly understand reality.

To do this, it is essential we develop our ability to be mindful and concentrated. These are the arts of directly touching life in the here and now, and they are also the practices of the Jedi, the way they live in touch with the living Force.

We turn now to *The Dharma of Star Wars*—and the Jedi art of mindfulness and concentration.

SECTION I:
THE DHARMA *of* STAR WARS

I THE JEDI ART

of MINDFULNESS AND CONCENTRATION

"Don't center on your anxieties, Obi-Wan,
keep your concentration here and now where it belongs."

"But Master Yoda said I should be mindful of the future."

"But not at the expense of the moment,
be mindful of the living Force, young Padawan."

JEDI MASTER QUI-GON JINN AND JEDI PADAWAN OBI-WAN KENOBI
IN "THE PHANTOM MENACE"

THE STAR WARS EPIC begins, in this dialogue, with mindfulness and concentration. In Episode I, *The Phantom Menace,* Jedi Master Qui-Gon Jinn advises his Padawan, Obi-Wan Kenobi, on these practices while the two are aboard the Trade Federation Droid-Control Ship representing the Galactic Republic as ambassadors of peace. Obi-Wan gives voice to his concern about and wariness of a far-off disturbance in the Force. Qui-Gon, sensing his apprentice is lost in the future and not grounded in the here and now, councils him to practice the Jedi art of mindfulness and concentration. Mindfulness and concentration are also the beginning and end of the practices handed down from Siddhartha, and that came to be known as Buddhism.

These two practices are essential steps along the path of spiritual freedom and happiness; they are methods for cultivating understanding, which is necessary to love ourselves, others, and life; and they are vital elements for being in touch with the living Force, for living in the present. If we are to be truly alive we must touch life deeply here and now because there is no life outside this moment. The past is gone and the future is not yet come. We must stop ourselves from being swept away by thoughts of the past or worries about the future. Just as Qui-Gon Jinn advises young Obi-Wan, we too should keep our attention "here and now where it belongs."

Yet it is difficult to remain in the present. We become caught in the memories of our past mistakes and lost in fantasies about future triumphs, and in so doing we lose the joy available in the present. In the time of the Buddha his disciples were known to be exceptionally joyful and even radiant. It was a striking sight: simple monks, residing in the wilderness and eating very little, yet so luminous and serene. When asked how this came to be, the Buddha said, "They do not repent the past, nor do they brood for the future. They live in the present. Therefore they are radiant. By brooding over the future and repenting the past, fools wither away like green reeds cut down."

When we do not waste our energy brooding and repenting (or whining like Luke Skywalker!), we are freer and have more opportunities to stop and smell life's roses—and when we do we become aware that there are a lot more roses around us than we ever imagined. In every moment countless small joys bloom, but too often we take them for granted. The Star Wars movies, food, running water, and life itself are just a few examples of the simple joy present right now. Living as Qui-Gon, remaining concentrated and mindful in the here and now, opens our eyes to these wonders, brings us happiness, and in itself relieves much of our daily suffering.

In regard to his ministry the Buddha said, "I teach only suffering and the cessation of suffering." He was not interested in abstract philosophical theorizing. He found of little importance such questions as "Is the soul one thing and the body another?" "Is the world beginningless?" and "Will the universe have an end?" To him, pondering these was wasted time because it did nothing to cure the problem plaguing the world—the problem of suffering.

This focus on suffering may appear morbid—like a kind of unhealthy fascination with the dark side of life—but truly it is the opposite. It is pragmatic, vital and deeply freeing. Suffering is a fact of life—and indulging in speculative cerebral processing about life and death serves us little when our Jedi master dies or when our own death approaches. Honestly recognizing suffering is a necessary first step toward transcending it. And transcending suffering is possible if we begin with the teaching of Qui-Gon and practice the Jedi art of mindfulness and concentration.

Living as Qui-Gon instructed, in touch with the present moment, we may observe our present suffering and the causes and conditions that give rise to it. When we look closely, we begin to realize we suffer because of previously unexamined views, beliefs, attitudes, and habits. Mindfulness is a way of watching our mind in order to discover the different ways we create suffering.

One way we create suffering is by playing the "Should Game": we tell ourselves we or the world "should be" different. We think we should not be the way we are or the world should not be as it is. We tell ourselves we should be better people and criticize ourselves for out shortcomings. "I should be kinder, calmer, and more generous," is the way I typically play the Should Game.

There is nothng wrong with improving myslef, but when I start playing the Should Game I make my life a struggle. I struggle against myself. I judge myself and ridicule myself—and right there suffering arises. When I latch on to my "should" thoughts I take myself away from the present joys into an imaginary future world where I will be "better"—but never *happier,* because the Should Game can never be won, and the mind that plays it is never satisfied.

The Should Game, pride, and habitual patterns of suffering are not things we try to get rid of or banish from our psyche. They are not the dark side's agents of evil that we set out to destroy. They are merely aspects of ourselves that we may observe in the way Qui-Gon instructed Obi-Wan. At the heart of the Jedi art of mindfulness and concentration one can find the ancient Greek maxim "Know thyself." When we know ourselves we understand why we suffer, and knowing this eases a great amount of our pain. Mindfulness is the method for coming to know who we are. Mindfulness does not judge or reject the causes of suffering; it is simply aware. And with awareness of the causes of suffering we can learn to let go of them.

The Should Game does not in itself cause suffering. Suffering is created when we *buy into* the game—when we are continuously and dogmatically convinced we need to be something more than what we are. Mindfulness helps us see the idea of "should be" or "should not be" surface in our mind, and then, if we are wise, instead of perpetually trying to remake ourselves or others we simply *do not buy into those ideas*. The Buddhist term for this is *letting go*.

IN "A NEW HOPE" Luke Skywalker races his X-wing along the Death Star trench preparing to fire the proton torpedoes that would destroy the Empire's ultimate weapon. Fiddling with his ship's targeting computer, Luke hears Obi-Wan Kenobi's voice, "Use the Force, Luke." Unsure of himself Luke dismisses the command and returns to what he believes he *should* be doing: targeting his mechanical scope for the crucial shot. Then the voice speaks again, "Let go, Luke."

When we let go of the things we believe we need—a targeting computer, the new XP-38 Landspeeder, the DVD player with a five-disc changer, or any of the other myriad crutches of life—we open up to infinite possibilities. Luke let go and allowed himself to touch the Force in the present moment—and of course we know the outcome of his shot! Luke was one with the Force at that instant, fully focused on his one present-moment task. He would not have succeeded in his mission of destroying the Death Star without letting go.

We can also let go of the things we chronically cling to as truth, the things we stubbornly grasp as important, and the things we habitually hang onto as necessary. To remain attached to ideas and habits, mechanical devices and protocol, is to limit ourselves and possibly set ourselves down the path of suffering. To release attachments to these things means they become *choices* we are free to make rather than addictions we blindly follow. But to do that we need to develop what both the Buddha and the Jedi call *mindfulness*.

The method for developing mindfulness is easy to understand—yet surprisingly difficult to put into practice. The practice requires us to focus our awareness on what is going on within us and around us at this instant—being mindful of the living Force. When we read this book, we know we are reading this book. If our thoughts drift off to what we are going to eat for dinner, or what events we have scheduled tomorrow, or what we would do if we had Jedi powers, then we are not reading mindfully. If you are reading, be aware you are reading. When standing, sitting, or lying down, be aware you are standing, sitting, or lying down.

Mindfulness is the energy that shines light on all we see and all we do. It is awareness of what is happening right now. Mindfulness supports *concentration*—the art of precisely and deeply focusing one's attention on an object or task at hand—and together the two bring us into direct contact with reality, where insight and understanding are born.

Being mindful and staying present with life and its instant-to-instant shifts is much more difficult than it sounds. We may try to comply with Qui-Gon's advice, yet mindfulness and concentration are not light switches we can simply turn on. You cannot just decide to be mindful and be done with it, living forever in deep awareness. But do not take my word for it—try it for yourself. After reading this paragraph put the book down, stand up, get a glass of water, and drink it. Then come back.

BACK? Okay. Now, try to recall as you walked to the cupboard, got yourself a glass, and proceeded to fill it, did your thoughts ever drift away? Were you telling yourself stories about the ease or difficulty of the task? Were you *thinking about* being mindful or actually *being* mindful? Did you notice the sound of your steps and tactile experience of holding the glass? Or did you lose yourself in fantasy?

If your experience was anything like most people, then you see that remaining mindful of each present activity—walking, reaching, grabbing, holding, pouring, breathing, drinking, and so on—as it occurs is much harder than, say…successfully navigating an asteroid field! And what are the odds of that? Well, we don't have See-Threepio here to tell us these things, but needless to say it is not easy. (Probably harder than "approximately three thousand, seven hundred and twenty to one"!) So, if you were not as mindful as you would like to be just notice that thought and do not get down on yourself: most of us are not masters of Jedi mindfulness—*yet.*

It is difficult to be mindful because many of us have lived unmindfully for years and even decades. Yoda's words about Luke in *The Empire Strikes Back* can easily be applied to us: "Never his mind on where he was. What he was doing." Likewise, our minds are rarely in touch with where we are and with what we are doing. And in this way we have accumulated many years of living without mindfulness—doing one thing mechanically while thinking about another—and this habit of living distractedly has become ingrained in us.

In fact, the habit of living distractedly is so strong in many of us it has become like a runaway podracer pulling us along. We try to wrest back the controls, but the energy of the thing is too strong. We are swept away by the habit energy of distraction and carelessness, and before we know it we've crashed into the side of Beggar's Canyon, bringing hardship to ourselves and others.

To avoid such a catastrophe there are several ways to develop our mindfulness. One has already been mentioned: recognition of what you are doing at this very moment. Recognition is easy to achieve but hard to maintain from moment to moment. Fortunately there is a powerful tool that gives us a means of staying anchored to the present. That anchor is mindful breathing.

MINDFUL BREATHING is simply the practice of concentrating on the breath. With the inhalation, you know that you are breathing in. With the exhalation, you know you are breathing out. You follow the breath in with awareness as it goes in, and you follow it as it goes out. You notice that the breath is long or short when it is long or short. With mindful breathing you just notice the breath; you do not try to hold it or force it; you do not alter its rhythm or change its volume. Don't hold on to the idea that you should breathe a certain way. Simply become aware of the way your body naturally breathes.

As we focus on our breathing we discover that our mind does not easily stay attuned to our breath, but flies off in a million different directions. But through sustained effort and practice, the podracer of our mind—once flying away heedlessly—begins to slow down. We do not forcibly take hold of the podracer's controls to bring about this deceleration; rather it is with gentle mindfulness that the frenetic machine is ever so subtly coaxed into a state of ease.

LUKE SKYWALKER learned the art of mindful breathing on his first visit to Dagobah, in *The Empire Strikes Back*. While climbing up vines, dashing through the undergrowth, leaping logs and rocks, the young Jedi pupil, his master on his back, is being instructed on the dangers of the dark side of the Force. Luke's mind races with a thousand questions about the dark side: is the dark side stronger than the good side of the Force, how can he distinguish it from the good, and why can he not do certain things. Luke's questions come in such a rapid-fire manner that it is clear to Master Yoda Luke has lost touch with the here and the now. Noticing this, and sensing Luke's mind was running away from him, he brings the lesson to an end. "Nothing more will I teach you today," Yoda says. "Clear your mind of questions."

Often we have concerns about a future event or confusion about the way something works and our mind becomes lost in a labyrinth of questions, doubts, and plans. Aware of this tendency, Yoda stops Luke before he can become bewildered, rather than empowered, by his education and training. By directing Luke to clear his mind of questions, Yoda is instructing the boy to come back to the present moment—to return to his breath. Luke does as he is told and almost instantly he is visibly calmer.

EVERY DAY WE ACCUMULATE STRESS and

anxiety. This creates tension in the body and mind that can cause physical as well as mental and psychological maladies. The practice of mindful breathing as a way of calming mind and body is a powerful remedy for illness. It is simple to do and always at hand. We don't need a doctor's prescription for the medicine of mindful breathing! We can just turn our attention to the body's breath and notice the natural process of breathing. With the inhalation we silently say, "I am aware of my in-breath." As we exhale, "I am aware of my out-breath." Doing this, we can also learn to stop ourselves from blindly following misplaced emotions or ideas that so often create suffering.

I have said that mindful breathing is like an anchor that keeps us in the present moment. To take that analogy further we can imagine ourselves as boats. Without the anchor of mindfulness we will be swept away by waves of ideas and emotions, and our peace and stability will soon be dashed to bits. But making good use of our anchor, we can avoid being swept away. We can just watch the waves of emotion swell, break, and crash upon the shore. Waves rise and fall; that is their nature. This is called *impermanance*. Because we are anchored with mindfulness we do not get carried away by the waves and so we do not suffer or cause others to suffer. Yet because we have not yet mastered the Jedi art of mindfulness, we so often unthinkingly lift our anchor of mindfulness and catch the next great swell of urgency just because we believe we have to.

Chasing one thing after another is how most of us live. We ride each new idea into dissatisfaction, and then to escape its drudgery we catch another and another and another—perpetually meeting dissatisfaction. We can call this the "If Only" game. *If only* I had a better job, more money, a girlfriend like Natalie Portman *then* I would be happy. But the If Only game does not produce happiness, only the endless cycle of chasing it.

THE JEDI PRACTICE OF MINDFULNESS and

concentration helps us discover ourselves and the ways we create suffering. It is a method of observation, not a means of becoming a different person. We do not need to *become* anything, only observe the impermanent nature of our feelings, thoughts, and the world itself. Observation reveals to us when our actions lead to suffering and when they lead to freedom, and that gives us the wisdom to make choices that will keep us off the path of the dark side.

Throughout Star Wars we see the Jedi practicing mindfulness and concentration, and as they do they come to better understand themselves, the galaxy, their own personal suffering, and the dark side within—the subject of our next chapter.

THE DARK SIDE WITHIN

"There's something not right here. I feel cold, death."

*"That place...is strong with the dark side of the Force.
A domain of evil it is. In you must go."*

LUKE SKYWALKER AND MASTER YODA
IN "THE EMPIRE STRIKES BACK"

LUKE SKYWALKER scrabbles over the gantry, his body aching from the abuse it has sustained, his arm searing in pain at the point it abruptly stops just above the wrist. He reaches the edge of the gantry, but there is no escape from his foe. He turns to face him, and with four words Darth Vader rips away the false reality Luke has lived with all his life.

"I am your father."

Shock and dismay overwhelm the Jedi pupil. Luke's world suddenly turns upside-down and reveals a side that is too much to bear. Unable to face it, awash in suffering he lets go of the gantry and falls.

Many of us have experienced moments in our lives of deep, overwhelming suffering. Moments—or even days—when our whole world is blotted out by suffering, when our problems seem to be the only thing that exists, and when, like Luke, even death seems preferable to facing them.

Birth, old age, sickness, death, sorrow, pain, grief, despair, association with what we don't like, and separation from what we do are all forms of suffering. The simple fact is that suffering is a part of life.

To understand this better we can examine suffering in several different forms. One form is ordinary suffering. This is the pain that one typically associates with the body—birth, sickness, physical injuries, bodily pain, and the like. Luke being pummeled by Force-hurled objects in Cloud City, Leia receiving a Stormtrooper blaster shot to her shoulder, Anakin losing half his arm to a charismatic, saber-swinging warmonger, Padmé being ripped across the back by a bloodthirsty nexu, and Lando having the life squeezed out of him by a wrathful Wookiee are each examples of ordinary suffering.

A second form of suffering is that associated with change. Life is perpetually changing. Because of this we are constantly gaining and losing things that bring us happiness. With old age we lose the vigor of youth. The joy we feel when we buy the Episode I COMMTECH™ Reader disappears when we discover the blasted thing doesn't even work. The impermanence of life means that even when something good happens it later passes away. After Luke Skywalker destroys the first Death Star in *A New Hope,* there is elation in the rebels' hidden fortress. It is not long, however, until their joy turns to fear and they are forced to flee the wrath of the Empire to the ice world of Hoth. The loss of a happy feeling is an example of suffering of the second form.

Another form of suffering can be described as frustration. When we are forced to be in a situation we do not like or if we cannot do what we would like to do, we may become frustrated. In *Attack of the Clones,* Anakin Skywalker feels smothered by his exacting master. He accuses Obi-Wan of hindering his progress as a Jedi and even implies that the elder Jedi was to blame for his mother's death. Anakin is frustrated because he is not able to do what he wants to do and he cannot entirely control the events in his life.

When we are not fully and mindfully aware of frustration we often act in ways that are unskillful and even destructive. Anakin's frustration is not cared for with Jedi mindfulness and thus it fosters a relentless quest to control not only events immediate to him but also the galaxy itself. This ultimately produces Darth

Vader. As a creature of the dark side, Vader—like everything he touches—suffers immensely.

Now let us consider the dark side of the Force itself: The dark side represents an energy that we may regard as another form of suffering. The dark side manifests as anger, fear, aggression, and hatred. Master Yoda says in *The Phantom Menace,* "Fear leads to anger, anger leads to hate, hate leads to suffering." This may be true, but we can take Yoda's teaching one step farther and say *attachment* to fear, anger, and hate *is* suffering; and fear, anger, and hate do not arise one from the other, but from confusion within our own mind.

When we are attached to the dark side we suffer and those around us suffer as well. When our anger overwhelms us and we can't seem to let it go we can do or say things that hurt our friends and loved ones.

WE ONLY NEED TO LOOK AT ANAKIN and his slaughter of the Tusken Raiders in *Attack of the Clones* to see how synonymous the dark side and suffering are.

Anakin is overcome with grief when his mother died—an understandable and appropriate reaction! But that grief transforms into hatred for her murderers and drives Anakin to slay them all, "not only the men, but the women and the children too."

We might imagine that acting out our anger will free us from it, but in Anakin's case his rage is not quelled by destroying the Tuskens—it is *intensified* by it. Anakin failed to mindfully care for his sorrow and anger and instead repressed it, and this begot the dark side, magnifying the suffering within him. Later, we see his suffering continues to grow when, at the Lars homestead, he confesses his actions to Padmé. Anakin is overwhelmed with misery. His intensified rage explodes, he throws a tool, and screams wild accusations before finally breaking down and weeping.

WE DON'T GET RID OF SUFFERING by acting out our

anger or throwing a tantrum. In fact, the very effort of "getting rid" of suffering is just another kind of suffering. It is a mistake of the mind, as we will see later. Suffering is a natural experience of all humans—Jedi, Buddhists, and everyone else too. However, we can lessen the intensity of our suffering by facing it with clear mindfulness so it does not overwhelm us as it does Anakin.

We've discussed suffering in terms of bodily pain and other physical effects such as aging. We've seen suffering manifest in the form of mental anguish like with the death of a loved one or the frustration of dealing with a strict teacher. But suffering is not always catastrophic or life changing. It is also present in littler, subtler things. Among its specific manifestations, we can see suffering in a broad, indefinite sense that connotes meanings of insubstantiality, imperfection, and impermanence. This provides us with a definition of suffering that indicates a general dissatisfaction with life.

It is that "I can't quite put my finger on it, but something is not right" feeling. It is restlessness, malaise, anxiety, angst. It is the meandering search through life that leads us from place to place, job to job, partner to partner, hoping to find that proper fit, that missing element that will make everything as it should be. It is that feeling that our happiness will occur sometime in the future, perhaps when we have completed school, gotten married, or raised our children. It is dissatisfaction with the here and the now.

Recognizing that suffering is an undeniable fact of life does not mean that we are agreeing with See-Threepio's grouse that "We seem to be made to suffer. It's our lot in life." It is not our lot in life, because there is a way out, a way to transform suffering into peace, joy, and freedom.

In order to transform suffering we need to understand it. Suffering is not an enemy to fight, suppress, or run from—or to hunt down and kill. It is an aspect of ourselves that we can come to appreciate if we have patience, courage, and compassion. The first step toward transformation is *recognition*.

TO UNDERSTAND AND FREE OURSELVES from suffering we have first to recognize it. Following Qui-Gon's advice and being mindful in our daily life allows us to be aware of the presence of suffering as it manifests.

For instance, we may notice that frustration arises in us as we wait in a long line at the movies. Typically we are unconsciously frustrated, and that feeling sweeps us deep into suffering. Our jaw clenches and muscles tighten. The people around us become annoying. The child playing in the queue grates our nerves. We create a lot of suffering in the line because things are not the way we want them to be. As we get more and more aggravated, if we are not careful, the podracer of our mind will pull us into disaster. This is when we need to practice mindful breathing to bring awareness to our suffering and calm our mind so we may look deeply at our thoughts and fully recognize our state of mind, rather than be bullied around by it.

Recognition of our state of mind—in this case frustration—stems the tide of suffering. Not recognizing our state of mind is like running around with a blast shield over our eyes—we are bound to get hurt and to hurt others. So, retracting the blast shield means we recognize that we are momentarily blinded by our frustration, and this recognition instantly mitigates our suffering and leads to the second step of transformation—*acceptance*.

AFTER RECOGNIZING the presence of frustration in us we may become angry or disappointed with ourselves for being so frustrated with a simple thing like standing in line. But, neither of these reactions can help us. They only deepen our present suffering. Instead of adding to the unpleasantness of frustration it is more beneficial to accept it. It is okay that we become frustrated. Frustration, anger, hatred, and sadness are part of life. We cannot avoid them or dispel them. They are not the cause of suffering; our aversion to them is. Trying to suppress, run from, or ignore frustration is simply a waste of time (and potentially a cause of more intense misery!). If we accept the presence of frustration we can transform it into understanding.

There are two reasons why it is beneficial to accept frustration and other such difficulties. The first is because difficulty is part of life—and denying that fact would simply do no good. It is important for our happiness that we accept the whole of life, even the dark side and the parts we would rather reject.

Our natural tendency is to run away from difficult feelings

and situations—but running away is just another form of suffering. Until we can learn to sit—or stand (in line), as the case may be—patiently with what we do not like we can never be free. The second reason acceptance is important is that frustration offers us an opportunity to *look deeply,* and this is the third step of *transformation.*

LOOKING DEEPLY means we investigate our frustration. We look to see the causes and conditions that have given rise to it. This is what Anakin fails to do after his mother dies. His attachment to the way he wanted things to be, to his sorrow, and to his burgeoning rage overwhelms him—and then he massacres the Tusken Raiders.

Unlike Anakin, we can save ourselves from regrettable actions by looking deeply. On the day we are waiting in line for tickets we may have many other things to do. Standing there is costing us the time we need to do those things, and so we become frustrated. Looking deeply can show us that the cause of our frustration may be an overbooked schedule. Perhaps we have too many obligations in our life, and we are feeling weighed down. Or perhaps we are frustrated because life—the reality of this moment in line—is not the way we think it should be, and we can't accept it as it is. Either way, discovering the conditions that have contributed to our frustration allows for the opportunity of *insight*.

INSIGHT IS THE FINAL STEP toward transformation. We cannot make insight happen, but mindfulness, recognition, acceptance, and looking deeply allow it to occur naturally in its own time. Our insight may be that we have created too much work in our life. If we can find a way to lessen the burdens we have placed on ourselves then we will have more time to spend waiting when life requires we wait. And we will not feel frustrated standing in line. But our insight may go deeper. We may realize that this lame, tedious line complete with all its vexing facets is nothing more and nothing less than the reality of our life in all its glory. There is nothing else we can do, no where else we can go that is more complete than *being right here waiting in line.*

Yet recognizing, accepting, and looking deeply at suffering is not always easy. Sometimes suffering is much more elusive and darker than feeling frustrated in line. Other times suffering can be too painful to look at. For many of us there are aspects of ourselves that we do not want to know and that we would prefer did not exist.

Anakin suffers in *Attack of the Clones* when he cannot accept his "weaknesses" and blames himself for failing to save his mother. When we are confronted by our own "weaknesses" and "negative" elements we usually do our best to avoid them. We find ways to distract ourselves by turning on the television, broaching idle conversation, or drifting into fantasy. Such diversions help us to forget our worries, but they cannot bring us the liberation from suffering that is necessary for true happiness. That can only be found if we are willing to accept our suffering and take the time to carefully examine it.

When the Buddha looked deeply he discovered that suffering has no external cause, but is the product of our own ignorance and attachments. We typically see other people, organizations, or events as the source of our suffering. We think "if only" the world would conform to our ideals we could be happy. So we try to remake our friends and our family, or get rid of the things we do not like. But this course of action can never be successful.

CONSIDER LUKE'S EXPERIENCE in *The Empire Strikes Back*. Luke believes Darth Vader is the source of much of the galaxy's problems. He thinks if only he can get rid of Vader the galaxy will be relieved of a great deal of suffering—that's why he does not hesitate to attack the Dark Lord in the cave on Dagobah.

Let us recall that scene.

Luke has just finished a training exercise with Master Yoda when he turns a wary eye on a dark cave beneath a huge, black tree.

"There's something not right here. I feel cold, death," he says in a halting voice.

"That place," replies Yoda, referring to the cave, "is strong with the dark side of the Force. A domain of evil it is. In you must go."

Yoda orders Luke into the cave to face the dark side residing there. The dark side is all the suffering in life. It is frustration, hatred, anger, and all the negative feelings and thoughts that come from within us. By going into the dark side cave Luke is penetrating his own nature on a quest to recognize himself and his suffering. Yoda knows that if Luke can confront the suffering within him with compassion and understanding he will do much to overcome whatever hold the dark side has on him. But Luke makes the same mistake many of us make in our lives: he mistakenly believes his suffering originates from a source outside himself. In this case, that apparent source is Darth Vader.

Out of the misty gloom of the cave's interior Darth Vader seems to appear. Luke ignites his lightsaber, and after a brief exchange of blows he defeats the Dark Lord of the Sith, separating his masked head from his body. Yet despite this apparent victory Yoda later calls Luke's experience in the cave a failure.

Luke fails because he is unable to recognize that the supposed source of his suffering—Darth Vader—is in fact himself. When Vader's mask explodes it does not reveal the monster Luke had expected. Instead Luke's own face lays in the darkness. He has not killed Darth Vader; he has attacked himself.

LUKE'S EXPERIENCE shows us that when we think the cause of our suffering is something "out there" we are setting ourselves up for failure and greater suffering. Suffering comes from within us; it is a product of our mind—that was the crucial insight of the Buddha. Yet to discover this for ourselves we need to find time in our daily life to be quiet so we can begin to recognize the suffering in us, accept it, and examine it carefully to find how we created it. This is the practice of meditation that we see the Jedi do throughout the Star Wars series, and it is the only way we can transform our suffering. If we blame others or attack our suffering like Luke does, we lose the opportunity to take care of it.

He who sees suffering sees also the arising of suffering, sees also the cessation of suffering, and sees the path leading to the cessation of suffering. If we can see suffering we will come to see the cessation of it.

To "see" in this case means to understand. To understand suffering we need to see ourselves. This is Yoda's intent in sending Luke into the cave—for Luke to discover himself. But Luke does not like what he sees there (his dark-side nature) and so he attacks it. Luke imagines Darth Vader to be the cause of suffering, and he thinks by killing him he could kill it. In reality Luke is battling himself.

Of course, in the Stars Wars universe Darth Vader is responsible for harming many, many people. He makes millions suffer, and it is natural to think that if we remove him we remove suffering. We would certainly be wise to somehow stop Vader from harming more people, but most of the suffering that truly plagues us in reality is the suffering of hatred, fear, and anger *in our own mind*. This is what Luke actually faces in the cave and what he erroneously believed originated from Darth Vader.

SUFFERING IS UNIVERSAL. All species suffer. Please understand that your suffering (including such afflictions as hated, jealousy, and humiliation) is not a personal failure, specific only to you or only to some people. It is something we *all* share. If a Jedi is wise, and follows the words of Qui-Gon, he will watch his suffering in mindfulness to see how it manifests, but he will not attach to it as a permanent aspect of himself but will learn from it and grow.

If we can learn to see suffering for what it is, a fleeting phenomenon rooted in our own misperception, rather than a personal fault, we will no longer feel motivated to destroy it. We will no longer fear to face it, and once it is faced we will be able to *embrace it with mindfulness.* Embracing it means we do not ignore or reject the suffering, but that we enter it fully and mindfully into our consciousness. We become completely aware of the suffering.

It is not helpful to hate or judge suffering. It is much more prudent to treat it as Too-Onebee, Emdee-one, or some other conscientious medical droid cares for an injured patient. Being kind to our suffering in this way can be a difficult thing to do because our hatred or frustration is often very ugly. Like a blemish on our face we are embarrassed of it and do not want it to be seen. So we cover it up or hide away. Or it can be repulsive like some slimy, green thing slinking around Dagobah. That is why it is helpful to see our suffering as a wounded rebel, perhaps recovering from a terrible battle with Darth Vader. We look at our patient of suffering: Is he hemorrhaging? Is there in infection in his wound? Has he gone into shock? This line of inquiry helps us heal his injuries and reduce his discomfort.

So, when we suffer we use our mindfulness to recognize and embrace it, and to follow a line of inquiry similar to the one we used with the wounded rebel—looking deeply to discover the nature of our pain and the conditions that have come together to make it surface.

IN "A NEW HOPE"

Luke is unhappy because he cannot leave Tatooine. He suffers fits of anger and hopelessness because that desolate place does not offer him the excitement he longs for. We can say that Luke's dissatisfaction with his life on Tatooine is the result of three conditions: his apparent imprisonment there, his desire to leave, and his attachment to that desire. If we remove one condition—for example, Luke's attachment to his desire to leave—he would no longer be miserable. Therefore, attachment to the desire to be someplace else is a necessary condition of Luke's suffering. It is not important to judge Luke's attachment as good or bad, right or wrong, but only to recognize that it *is* a condition of his suffering. To perceive the conditions of our unhappiness is to understand why we suffer. With understanding comes the ability to let go of the ideas, impulses, and attachments that bind us to the dark side—then our choice to leave or stay on Tatooine won't be bound up with a lot of angst and mental torment.

To build a fire certain conditions are necessary. We need fuel, heat, and oxygen. Without all three of these elements there cannot be fire. The same is true with suffering. Certain conditions are necessary for one to suffer.

FACING SUFFERING AND DARK SIDE WITHIN US

takes a great deal of courage and compassion. It takes courage because it is much easier to find solace in entertainment than to investigate our pain and sorrow. The entertainment itself is not bad in any moral sense, but it can be harmful if it prevents us from facing our suffering and transforming it.

Setting the PlayStation game controller down, turning off the DVD player, and simply walking peacefully in nature is an opportunity for us to shed pent-up emotions and gather strength to embrace our dark side elements. Taking five, ten, or thirty minutes a day to just stop and be quiet can have a remarkable impact on our happiness and our understanding of suffering. We can also emulate the Jedi and find time in our daily life to practice sitting meditation so we can look deeply into the causes and conditions that give rise to suffering.

It takes compassion to transform suffering because to really do the work of liberating ourselves from its bonds we must be patient and kind to ourselves, and this is rarely our natural disposition. Our tendency to avoid suffering and our misunderstanding of its causes has created a lot of confusion in our life. Because we are confused we mishandle suffering. We blame others or may even berate ourselves when we are unhappy or in a foul mood. In these times it is helpful to remember that we are human and prone to mistakes.

In *Return of the Jedi*, Luke turns himself over to the Empire because he senses good still remains in Darth Vader and thinks he can help him to turn back to the good side of the Force. If we emulate Luke's compassion for Vader, a man responsible for the death of millions, then we can have compassion for and forgive ourselves our foibles.

THE DARK SIDE IS PART OF EVERYONE. And so is

suffering. The presence of the dark side does not in itself make one evil, and suffering is not in itself a weakness. Feelings of hatred and envy are not failures. These things are merely aspects of life that manifest when conditions are appropriate. The Jedi practice of mindfulness allows us to understand these conditions, and understanding eases suffering. But to understand the causes and conditions of suffering we need courage and compassion to face it. We also need a lot of time and space. Meditation—practicing as we've seen the Jedi do—is a method of providing us with that time and space. It is also a way of removing the shroud of the dark side—the topic of our next chapter.

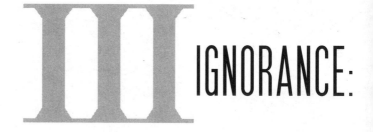

III IGNORANCE:

THE SHROUD *of* THE DARK SIDE

*"You and the Naboo form a symbiont circle.
What happens to one of you will affect the other.
You must understand this."*

OBI-WAN KENOBI
IN "THE PHANTOM MENACE"

O BI-WAN TELLS US the Naboo and the Gungans are united in a "symbiotic circle"—but this kind of relationship is not limited to the two sentient races of a distant world. All things are in a state of symbiosis, a state of interdependence with one another. In fact, the whole of reality itself is inclusively united. This fact is very difficult to see because we are often blinded by our own ignorance, our own dark side shroud that clouds our vision of reality.

Ignorance is at the root of our suffering, and it is the single greatest hindrance to a life of freedom and joy. Out of ignorance comes the false idea of "self." This is the notion that creatures and things—for example, Tuantuans, human beings, Wookiees, and even the stars themselves—have an independent existence separate from all other things. From this ignorance arises such forms of suffering as fear of death, hatred of others, and war.

The idea of a separate self is false because it ignores the true nature of reality, of Obi-Wan's "symbiont circle." That true nature we can call "emptiness." To be empty in this sense means to be empty of a separate self. We commonly think we are independent entities. We believe our existence is separate from others, but if we look carefully at ourselves we will discover we are made up entirely of "non-us" elements. Our body is made up of our parents and ancestors, oxygen, water, and food. Our thoughts are made up of the books we have read, the culture we live in, the education we have received, the movies we obsess over. We are not separate from these things but made up of them and dependent on them for our existence. (Can you imagine the nature of your existence without

Star Wars? How different your thoughts and outlook would be?) That is the meaning of emptiness.

For many of us the notion that we are not separate from the books we have read or the stars way up in the sky is peculiar—to say the least!

TO BETTER UNDERSTAND Obi-Wan's symbiont circle, and

to better demonstrate what is meant by emptiness, let us consider the example of a table.

The table in question is made of wood, and we know wood comes from trees. Looking at it we recognize this right away. But what we may not recognize is the presence of the forest, the soil, the rain, the sun, the lumberjack, the lumber mill, the carpenter, and many, many other things in the table. Why would we? After all, a table is just a table. But if we follow the table back in time we will discover that these things all played a part in its life, its very existence.

We can begin the genealogy of a table from when it was a full-grown tree (but take a moment to reflect that this is not a *beginning,* just an arbitrary starting point—because that tree has its own genealogy stretching into the infinite past). The tree is in a forest—say, on the moon of Endor. The tree has grown tall and strong over many years on a diet of air, sunlight, water, decomposed leaves, and other things. Without the air, sunlight, water, and decomposed leaves the tree could not exist. The tree needs these basic elements to survive. Therefore, the air, sunlight, water, and decomposed leaves are in the tree.

We can find other things in the tree as well. An Ewok may grow old, die, and be buried near her favorite tree—the very same tree we are now discussing. As her body decomposes it nourishes the tree. Through the process of decomposition the Ewok becomes part of the tree, and if we look closely we can see her there.

Imagine we are on Endor and we wish to construct a table for enjoying meals. We gather some friends, borrow a few tools from the furry natives, and fell a tree. We take the tree, shave off its bark, chop it up, shape it down, and produce a magnificent piece of furniture. The table would not have come into existence without our work, the axe we borrowed from the little furball locals, or the carpentry tools we used. It would not exist without the sun, rain, air, and decomposition process that helped the tree grow.

Looking at the finished table it may be difficult to see all these different things in it, but they are there. If the rain had not fallen, there would be no tree, and subsequently, no table. Without the rain there is no table. If we had not had parents who loved us enough to feed us and keep us safe we would not have been there to cut down the tree. Without our parents there would be no table. Supposing by tradition we ate our meals on the ground, there would be no motivation for building a table to eat dinner on. Had all these conditions not come together in just such a way, the table would have never existed. What this means is all aspects of life, from the rain to the table, to custom and tradition, are *interdependent*. And when we look deeply into their empty nature we find that they have penetrated one another—that they are *interpenetrated*.

If you lean three reeds against one another they can stand. Remove one and they all fall. Take away the Ewok's axe or the food that gave us the strength to do our work and the chain of events that produced the table would collapse.

THE SHROUD OF THE DARK SIDE obscures the full

depth of circumstances that constitute life and does not allow us to perceive the chain of events that connects us with the world—and so we suffer. We suffer because we assume we can find happiness only in certain things and fail to see that the things we love are not confined to a particular time and space but are all around us.

We love Star Wars. But Star Wars is not restricted just to the movies, books, and merchandise. Star Wars is in our hearts and minds. It is in the child who dreams of becoming a Jedi. It is in the merch-dealer who dresses up as a Stormtrooper every Halloween. It is even in the Star Wars fans' ancient rivals, those dastardly Trekkies. If we look carefully we will see that what we love is in children, antiques, and, yes, Klingons.

The dark side shroud also causes us to suffer because it leads us to believe we are independent from (rather than *inter*dependent with) the world around us. We may imagine we are separate from the forest, the air, and the earth. We think it does not matter that this forest is clear-cut, or that oil is dumped on the earth, or these toxins are released into the atmosphere. We may believe none of that will affect us because we fail to see the air, forest, and earth in us.

Looking deeply into ourselves we realize that we are entirely made of "nonself" elements. *Nonself elements* are things that we don't commonly recognize as being the essence of who we are, what this thing we call a self is. One of those elements, for instance, is air. It is a nonself element because we don't usually identify ourselves wholly with the air. Yet we are surrounded by air. Air is constantly flowing in and out of our lungs, and its oxygen is carried by our blood to our muscles allowing us to live—yet most of the time we are not even conscious of it. We take our breathing for granted. We take the air for granted. Yet without air, of course, we could not live.

Air is in us, but it is also in the trees of the forest. The forest helps purify the air, and without it we could not survive. If we see the air in ourselves and the air in the forest, then we know the forest is in us as well, and we will not want to clear-cut it.

Earth is also in us. Our flesh, the "crude matter" Yoda speaks of in *The Empire Strikes Back,* decays and turns to dust. Every time we scratch our arm, microscopic dead skin cells fall to the ground. When the body dies and decomposes the flesh returns to the soil, enriching it, helping plants and trees to grow. If the trees are fruit trees then they provide us with not only clean air but also apples, nectarines, and oranges. As we eat the fruit we also eat the fertile soil.

In *Attack of the Clones,* Anakin Skywalker complains about sand getting everywhere—and he doesn't know how right he was! Sand is in every molecule of our being, every molecule of a landspeeder, and in every planet. Earth is in the fruit, and it is in us as well. To dump toxic waste in the earth is to dump it on us.

The air, forest, and earth are alive in us, and without them we could not exist. Thus, a human being is made up of non–human-being elements and cannot exist without them. This is a seemingly simple concept, but one that we often overlook as we live out our individual lives. Please look at yourself to recognize the nonself elements present in you.

WHEN WE TALK ABOUT INTERDEPENDENCE we do not

say that for its survival the tree *needs* the rain. That would be *dependence;* that is, the tree would be *dependent on* the rain. Interdependence means *both* the tree needs the rain *and* the rain needs the tree. The tree helps keep the air fresh and clean for other beings to breathe. The tree does this by absorbing carbon dioxide from the air and returning oxygen to the atmosphere. This process helps preserve the balance of gases in the environment that is essential for air to carry water molecules skyward, cooling as it goes and becoming rain clouds. Without the work of the trees to help stabilize the atmospheric conditions there would be no rain.

Through the insight of interdependence we can see interpenetration. We see the rain is inside the Ewok and the Ewok is inside the rain. The two have penetrated one another. As we have discussed, the rain depends on the tree, and, in turn, the tree depends on the Ewok for his exhalation of carbon dioxide. The Ewok is in the rain in the form of carbon dioxide. Conversely, the Ewok depends on the tree for oxygen, and the tree depends on the rain for nourishment. The rain gives the tree sustenance, and the tree gives the Ewok oxygen. The rain penetrates the Ewok in the form of oxygen.

Understanding the world in the context of interdependence, interpenetration, and emptiness allows us to see past the surface of a thing to discover the whole universe within it. Gazing at the rain cloud we can see the tree and the Ewok. But if we look at the table we built merely as a flat hunk of wood supported by four thinner pieces of wood what we see can be very boring. We lose sight of the table's deeper wonder and take it for granted. Piercing its outer guise reveals so much more. The forest, our dead ancestors, the rain and sun, all come alive. This is a beautiful way to experience the world and one that can make life immensely captivating.

IF WE LIVED IN THE STAR WARS GALAXY and

looked at the world through the shroud of the dark side, we likely would fail to find anything captivating about Artoo Detoo. He would simply be one of perhaps millions of astromech droids. His model would be on every planet, in nearly every town and city. We would walk right past him, unaware of his presence. This is a shame because Artoo *is* a miracle; he is the entire universe in one squat, three-legged bucket of bolts.

In Artoo is Wedge Antilles—the X-wing pilot instrumental in destroying the second Death Star—who would not have been able to achieve his task had Bothan spies not discovered its secret location; those spies would not have been able to report their findings to the Rebel Alliance had the Alliance not escaped from the Empire's attack on Hoth, which could not have happened without See-Threepio identifying the signal sent by the probe droid to the Imperial fleet; Threepio himself would not have been on Hoth had he been destroyed when the first Death Star was primed to annihilate the fourth moon of Yavin, which would have happened had two proton torpedoes not hit the space station's reactor system and set off a chain reaction; that one-in-a-million-shot could not have been achieved by anyone save Luke Skywalker; Luke would not have been in that X-wing had Stormtroopers not killed his aunt and uncle, and they would not have been killed had certain vital information not come, albeit unknowingly, into their possession; that information—the technical readouts of the first Death Star— would not have reached them had Princess Leia not been part of the scheme to deliver them to the rebels; Leia herself would not have been born had her mother not met her father. Padmé could not have met Anakin had she not fled to Tatooine, and she would never have reached that desolate world had her ship been destroyed by the Trade Federation blockade surrounding her planet, and *that* most definitely would have occurred had her ship's shield generator not been restored at the last second by a little astromech droid we know as Artoo-Detoo.

Perceiving the incredible chain of events, the number of lives touched and fortunes changed by one action of a single astromech droid we start to get a glimpse of just how deeply connected the universe is. The above example, however, touches only one linear chain of events. Stepping back from Artoo we begin to see that each point of contact—the rebel fighters, the Bothan spies, the Trade Federation—has thousands of vectors of cause and effect running in myriad directions. Drawing back further we start to get an idea of a complex web connecting all things. In Buddhist philosophy this web is called *Indra's Net.*

INDRA'S NET is an image used to illustrate the teaching of emptiness, the insight of Obi-Wan's "symbiont circle." Indra's net describes reality as stretching infinitely in all directions, with a jewel in every node of the net. Each jewel reflects every other jewel, and within each the reflections are compounded, creating reflection upon reflection into infinity. Standing at any point on Indra's Net we and everything else are reflected limitlessly. The Net of Indra reveals to us that when we look at Artoo we are also looking at proton torpedoes, Imperial probe droids, moisture farmers, economic embargoes, and the infinite number of things that comprise the entire universe—including us.

Indra's Net also exists *inside* of us. Each cell of our body is the accumulation of all history, and it is the container of infinite potential. The cell is the product of our parents, ancestors, and the food we have eaten, the air we have breathed, and the injuries we have endured. The history of the cell is one that is limitlessly interwoven with the fabric of reality. It is a history indistinguishable from our genetic ancestry. From time immemorial, that history has flowed like an endless river to this moment. We are the accumulation and continuation of that flow. We are also the active potential for its perpetual streaming.

IN "ATTACK OF THE CLONES" we discover that a single cell from the bounty hunter Jango Fett produced over a million clones. One cell of Jango's body, one cell of any human contains the active potential of a million lives! The enormity of sorrow, joy, love, and hate that can come out of one cell is truly vast and incredible.

In the Star Wars galaxy that one cell produced not only clones but also the decimation of the Jedi Order, the fall of the Republic, and the tyranny of the Empire. The clones were a vital instrument in Darth Sidious/Chancellor Palpatine's plans to seize the reins of galactic power. They were at the center of a war that killed many Jedi and weakened the Republic beyond recovery. Without the clones the light of peace and justice in the galaxy would never have been darkened by the shadow of the Empire.

The rise of the Empire and the subsequent terror and domination over the galaxy can be traced back to that single cell of the bounty hunter Jango Fett! Emptiness reveals the truth of reality. The truth is Jango Fett is not separate from the Empire, the Clone Wars, or the destruction of the Jedi. All of those things were present in him long before he was first cloned. This is because each cell of his body—each cell of all our bodies—is made up of *everything*.

Looking at one it is possible to see all. With careful consideration of Jango Fett it is possible to find star destroyers, TIE fighters, and the Death Star. This kind of deep recognition, grounded in understanding of interdependence and interpenetration, is called *right view.*

Right view—or right understanding—is one of the elements of the Buddha's Noble Eightfold Path—the path that transcends suffering. Right view is the highest wisdom, the insight that surpasses all concepts, beliefs, and points of view. It does not come from the intellect; it is not a conceptual grasping of some sort of knowledge. It cannot be acquired from reading any book about the ways of the Jedi, or about the way of the Buddha. It cannot be acquired by reading this book. Right view arises from our direct interaction with life. Direct interaction means mindfulness and concentration on what is happening right now. Only when we are fully present can we directly experience life.

Through direct experience the world reveals its empty and nonself nature. We see the universe as it is illustrated by Indra's Net. With right view we acquire the wisdom of the way things are in reality, and in this way we part the shroud of the dark side and transcend our ignorance.

OBI-WAN EXPRESSES RIGHT VIEW in *The Phantom Menace* when he informs Gungan leader Boss Nass, "You and the Naboo form a symbiont circle. What happens to one of you will affect the other. You must understand this." But because Boss Nass cannot see with right view, with the depth of Obi-Wan's perception, the Gungan leader does not understand the importance of the Jedi's statement.

It is natural to regard the world as Boss Nass did. We commonly think, "This is me. That is you." We draw boundaries separating ourselves from one another and think that this protects us from people's problems and troubles. But when we see through the shroud of the dark side we recognize our error. Boss Nass and the Gungans were forced to accept the inextricable ties they shared with their land-dwelling neighbors. War was brought on the Naboo by the droid army of the Trade Federation. That same force soon turned its destructive power on the Gungans. As the Naboo went, so went the Gungans. Removing the shroud of the dark side reveals the truth that indeed we all are symbiotically linked. It shows us that the suffering of others is our suffering; their joy is our joy.

If we fail to understand Obi-Wan's symbiont cycle, the unbreakable chain that links your suffering to my suffering produces more suffering. To blame you for my unhappiness is one way I can cause you harm while simultaneously creating grief for myself. Earlier we discussed the powerful scene from *The Empire Strikes Back* where Luke enters the dark side cave on Dagobah and attacks the phantasm of Darth Vader, yet after defeating his opponent, Luke discovers that it was not Vader he has destroyed, but himself. Let us return to that scene once more.

Before Luke enters the cave he turns to Yoda and asks, "What's in there?"

Yoda says, "Only what you take with you."

So what is it that Luke takes with him? Luke takes with him his ignorance, his misperception, his anger, his fear, and his aggression. But he does *not* bring with him Obi-Wan's deep perception of emptiness. Because of this Luke cannot see clearly enough to recognize the interdependent and interpenetrating nature of life and, instead, attacks the thing he wrongly identifies as his source of suffering—the evil Darth Vader.

When our understanding is shrouded by dark side ignorance we think the thing "out there" is the cause of our suffering. Luke cannot see himself in Darth Vader. He sees the dark side as existing only outside himself. But once Vader's helmet explodes Luke realizes the truth. He realizes that the dark side is in him, and he is in it. This is the insight Obi-Wan expresses to Boss Nass, the insight of emptiness.

IN OUR SOCIETY THERE IS CERTAINLY EVIL:

murders, kidnappings, and other horrible crimes, as well as the many subtler ways people can be cruel to each other. The typical conclusion is that these acts, when they are perpetrated by and happen to other people, have nothing to do with us. We believe they are the deeds of a deranged few and that their effects are limited to certain victimized individuals. But when we perceive the world as Obi-Wan does, we see that *we* are in the murderer and the murderer is in us. We are in he victim and the victim is us. We share our community with everyone living in it. If one person in our community is in so much pain that she feels compelled to kill another human being we need to investigate how our society operates and how, with our participation or our inaction, it has contributed to her unhealthy state of mind.

If our society promotes fiscal heath over mental health it may be coresponsible for the murder. If our society is structured in a way that promotes alcoholism and drug abuse it may contribute to the crimes associated with those addictions. If our society is more concerned with the next Harrison Ford movie then it is with its starving children then it may kill by neglect.

It is important that we practice mindfulness and look deeply into the nature of things in order to understand that the suffering in our society is not disconnected from us. If we support breweries by purchasing beer we are contributing to drunk driving and alcoholism in our society. If we work for companies that supply laborers to the Death Star construction project we are co-responsible for the destruction of Alderaan. When we peel back the mask of evil in our society and in the world we will find our own face staring back at us.

WHEN LUKE CONFRONTS what he thinks is Darth Vader in the dark side cave he is unable to see himself in the Dark Lord. We can call Luke's mistake the *mindset of discrimination*. The mindset of discrimination sees the world as separated, divided, and disconnected. It perpetuates misunderstanding and conflict in the world.

It is so easy to be confused when our understanding is shrouded by the dark side, and because of this, the mindset of discrimination is very strong in us. We may think it is not; we may believe we are tolerant and accepting of all people, but nonetheless we find it terribly difficult to love a violent racist. People who torment, torture, and murder others because of the color of their skin are very difficult to accept. The typical response is to draw a distinction between the racist and ourselves. "He is terrible," we think. "His hatred is disgusting. So it is alright for me to hate his hate." If we hate the racist's hatred, we become just like him. That is the way of ignorance.

With Obi-Wan's deep perception of emptiness, however, we know that the racist's hatred is based on ignorance. The racist does not understand that he is in the minority group and the minority group is in him. When he hates the minority group, he hates himself. This is very sad. We can forgive the racist and have compassion for him because we know he suffers. He suffers because he is trapped in the dark side of wrong thinking and is unable to love.

Hatred is never pacified by hatred, only when one acts with kindness is hatred pacified. If we offer the racist our understanding and kindness instead of our anger and distrust we will reduce the hatred in his heart.

In a deleted scene from *Attack of the Clones,* Senator Padmé

Amidala warns the Galactic Senate, "If you offer the separatists violence they can only show violence in return." This is true—and what's more, so does compassion propagate compassion. To change the heart of a person we need to offer him what we want from him. If we offer violence or hatred we will receive those things. If we offer kindness and compassion eventually we will receive kindness and compassion.

We do not live in this world independently. We share it with all beings, both murderers and holy men, Sith and Jedi. We exist in unity with rivers, forests, and the air. Mindfulness and concentration can part the shroud of the dark side and allow us to touch the reality of emptiness.

In the next chapter we will see how emptiness transcends the idea of self and the notion of birth and death.

IV ANAKIN, LEIA, AND

THE FIVE AGGREGATES OF SELF

"Master, moving stones around is one thing.
This is totally different."

"No! No different!
Only different in your mind.
You must unlearn what you have learned."

LUKE SKYWALKER AND MASTER YODA
IN "THE EMPIRE STRIKES BACK"

AT THE END OF "RETURN OF THE JEDI"

a dying Anakin Skywalker looks on his son for the first time with his unmasked eyes. Then very weakly he says, "Now…go, my son. Leave me."

Luke replies, "No. You're coming with me. I'll not leave you here. I've got to save you."

"You already have," says Anakin.

The idea that we are completely separate beings with a permanent character that is good or bad, lazy or generous is one of the false beliefs that shroud our understanding of reality. Luke does not adhere to that enshrouding belief when he looks at his father in this scene. While others see a man evil by nature, Luke recognizes the good in his father, and he knows that Vader can redeem himself.

Buddhism teaches that the idea of a permanent, independent self is false, that the human being is "empty"—made up only of the interaction of the universe and a unified part of the flow of life. So, what we commonly think of as a "self-sufficient" individual is in reality a combination of physical and mental elements called *the five aggregates*.

Aggregate is a word that refers to the collection of various elements into one particular formation. A simple example is lemonade, a drink we have all enjoyed and one that we might expect to find being sold on the lush world of Naboo or refreshing a desert-parched patron in Wuher's cantina in Mos Eisley. Whether it is found on Tatooine or on our world, lemonade is always the aggregate of lemon juice, sugar, and water. Likewise, every human being (and every Wookie, Jawa, or Mon Calamari!) is a formation made of the five aggregates of form, feeling, perception, mental formations, and consciousness. Each of these aggregates is the collection of various elements. For example, *form* (that is, the physical body itself) is made of other elements: water, hair, bone, and skin among many other things. Each aggregate is impermanent—never the same from one moment to the next. Because they are impermanent they cannot be said to be eternal. Furthermore, they are in no way independent because they are subject to the influence of life. This simply means that *form,* for example, is subject to the harsh conditions of Hoth and will freeze during the night if it is not ensconced in the warm carcass of a Tauntaun. Collectively, these five aggregates, these temporary impulses come together creating the human being—a thing that constantly changes as life changes. To better understand the impermanent and empty nature of the human being let us take a look at Anakin Skywalker.

The first thing we notice about Anakin is his body. His body is the aggregate *form.* We see the little, bright-eyed Anakin of *The Phantom Menace* and look on in surprise in *Return of the Jedi* when Luke removes the helmet and mask of Darth Vader to reveal a pale and disfigured shadow of that handsome boy. Over time the change in Anakin's body is quite evident. But the change in his body is not limited to the aging process or the lingering scars from his duel with Obi-Wan. Anakin's body, as well as our own, is continuously altering. It is sometimes tired, sometimes energetic. It is healthy now, and sick tomorrow. Its hair grows, its teeth fall out, and its size alters. The body constantly changes, but much of that change is so subtle that we fail to recognize that the body of one second ago is different from the body of right now.

Every moment we are alive we are soaking in life around us. Walking beneath the twin suns of Tatooine we take in the warmth and energy of their rays. The contact of sunlight on our skin causes a chemical reaction that alters us. The body of the moment before the sunlight struck it is different from the body of the moment after the sunlight touched it. We also soak in the air. Each inhalation of Cloud City's rarefied atmosphere brings air rich in oxygen into our lungs, and each exhalation returns air rich in carbon dioxide to the world. Sometimes the air we breathe carries a virus and we get sick. We change with the sun, and we change with the air.

Clearly our body is not permanent, but it is also not separate. It cannot survive without the sun or air. Nor could it exist without a father and mother. In fact, our body is an extension of our parents. If we reflect on our Endor table we realize that our body existed before our parents first met. We saw the table in the tree even while the tree was still standing, and in the tree we learned to see the whole of Endor.

If we look deeply into Anakin—in either of the first two Star Wars prequels—we see his daughter Leia. Leia's body is the present culmination of the genetic material that was handed down to Anakin through the unbroken chain of his ancestral lineage. Leia is not separate from Anakin or his ancestors. She is an extension of them, a continuation of them.

To see the body as an extension of its parents, the food it has ingested, the air, earth, sunlight, and everything else is to understand that it is not separate from these things. We know even now our bodies existed in our great, great grandmothers and that they hold the presence of our great, great granddaughters. So our existence is not trapped in our body. When the Buddha looked carefully into his existence he saw that it could not be found solely in the hands, arms, legs, feet, torso, and head of his body, but that it existed in his parents, the air, the sun—everywhere and in all beings. From that point on he no longer feared death.

We fear death because we think we are separate and distinct from the world around us and we believe our existence is depend ent upon our body. That fear is natural, and it vanquishes even the most hardened. Take, for example, the Emperor's scream of terror as he plummets down the central core shaft of the Death Star to his own death. But while the dark side of ignorance shrouded the Emperor's understanding of reality, others are not so blind to the truth. Qui-Gon Jinn meets death with no thought at all of himself, only compassionate concern for the galaxy. Unlike Qui-Gon, we often think that when our body dies we will be reduced to nothing, and we feel a great deal of anxiety over this. But if we look deeply into our bodies we would see that our bodies have *already* died. Each time our bodies breath there is a birth and death. The beginning of the inhalation is a kind of birth. Fresh air and other elements such as dust and fragrance enter our bodies, and for that instant they are different from the moment before. By the time the inhalation becomes the exhalation, the human being who breathed in has died—his lifespan complete. With each cycle of breath our bodies are born and die. (And also, with each arising and passing of a thought, the mind dies too!) Similarly, the process of birth and death can be observed in bodily cells. Cells are produced, or born, from the nutrients the body receives, and they die. New cells replace the dead ones, and in around seven years or so, the body has completely regenerated its cells—it is entirely new. Looking deeply in this way we realize we have lived through countless births and deaths without even knowing it. This insight may be of small comfort to Obi-Wan as he embraces Qui-Gon, holding his body for some time after Qui-Gon dies. And I know it was small comfort to me when I held my grandfather's hand after he passed, knowing that I would never again hear his seemingly endless stories or prune trees and pick fruit with him again. Like Qui-Gon, he is gone, and I miss him. But if we look at Obi-Wan we see qualities of Qui-Gon present in him. Yoda pointed this fact out, telling Obi-Wan, "Qui-Gon's defiance I sense in you." Similarly, when I look deeply at myself, I see that my grandfather is not truly gone; he is in me. He is my stubborn nature, my strange sense of humor, my sense of responsibility. My grandfather would not answer the phone were I to call his house, but I can hear his voice when I am quiet and attentive, and I can see his presence in my thoughts and actions even now as I type these words.

WE CAN LOOK AT PRINCESS LEIA and explore the

second aggregate of the human being, *feelings. Feelings* can refer to sensations arising from the body—such as hunger or pain—or they can refer to mental reactions of happiness, unhappiness, or indifference. If we observe our feelings we will see that they are continuously changing. In *A New Hope* Princess Leia feels anxious about her future and the future of the Rebel Alliance while she is held captive in the Death Star. She has seen Alderaan destroyed and does not know the fate of Obi-Wan Kenobi and Artoo Detoo—the droid who carried information vital to the survival of the rebellion. While sitting in her cell her anxiety quickly changes to puzzlement when an undersized Stormtrooper rushes in. The "Stormtrooper" removes his helmet and blurts, "I'm Luke Skywalker. I'm here to rescue you."

"You're who?" the Princess asks, her puzzlement deepening.

"I'm here to rescue you. I've got your Artoo unit. I'm here with Ben Kenobi."

Her bewilderment turns to guarded elation: "Ben Kenobi! Where is he?"

So: in a manner of seconds Leia's feelings go from anxiousness to confusion to joy. Feelings, like the body, are always shifting, and they change based on the contact the sense organs have with various phenomena.

When we see something, hear something, taste, touch, or smell something, we experience a feeling. That feeling can be pleasant, unpleasant, or neutral. The Buddha advised his disciples to be aware of their feelings as they arise in one context and fade away in another. Jedi Master Mace Windu advises young Anakin Skywalker in Episode I, "Be mindful of your feelings." Like Anakin, we must be mindful of our feelings as they arise in one context and fade away in another.

Conscious observation of the rise and fall of feelings produces the insight that feelings are in fact aggregates, things comprised of other elements. A feeling is an aggregate of the object we see, hear, taste, touch, or smell, the sense organ that is in contact with it, and our consciousness. All three of these are necessary for a feeling to arise. For example, to experience the joy of watching Star Wars, the movie must be playing, the eyes and ears must be able to receive information, and the mind must be attentive. Thus, the feeling of joy is dependent on the object seen and heard. The eyes and ears, the mind, and the images on the screen interpenetrate each other and produce our feelings of pleasure at watching Star Wars.

Understanding this, I know that I cannot identify myself as my feelings. My feelings do not encapsulate who I am; my love of

Star Wars, however strong, is not "me." Feelings are products of countless elements in the world coming together one minute and fading away the next—my feelings cannot exist without these elements. The same is true with the third aggregate, *perceptions*.

WHEN WE LOOK AT CHEWBACCA running around on

the screen we are perceiving Chewbacca. We might think that Chewie is outside of us, but that is not so. Chewie is part of us because he is the object of our *perception*. At the moment of perception subject and object are one. It is impossible to have a subject without an object. It is impossible to remove ourselves and retain Chewbacca. When the scene changes and Palpatine dominates the screen our perception changes, and then Palpatine is the object of our perception; Palpatine becomes part of us. So: *perceptions* are images that form in our mind as the result of the contact between the sense organs (sight, sound, smell, and so on) and the object perceived. Each time a sense organ makes contact with an object we have a new perception. And thus our perceptions are dependent on external phenomena and are impermanent—changing from moment to moment.

The perception produced by the interaction between a sense organ and an object can have a powerful impact on how we feel. When we see Chewie we experience positive feelings for our favorite Wookiee. When we see Palpatine we may experience disgust or trepidation over what sinister scheme he's cooking up. Much of how we feel about the object we perceive is wrapped up with our past experience, our sadness, our ignorance. In *The*

Empire Strikes Back, Leia watches the bounty hunter Boba Fett speed away from Cloud City with her love, Han Solo, encased in carbonite. Her perception may have been that she had lost Han forever.

In Buddhism it is said that "if there is perception, there is deception." In other words, most of our perception is erroneous; and this error is the cause of much of our suffering. Leia perceived that Han was gone, but this notion is grounded in an erroneous belief that Han could only be found in his *form*—the body frozen in carbonite.

In *A New Hope* Obi-Wan Kenobi leads his nascent learner, Luke Skywalker, in a training session aboard the *Millennium Falcon.* Luke uses his lightsaber to defend himself from small blasts emanating from a hovering seeker-droid. Wishing to expand the lesson, Obi-Wan places a helmet on Luke's head that completely covers his eyes. Luke does not hesitate to call this to Obi-Wan's attention. "With the blast shield down, I can't even see. How am I supposed to fight?"

"Your eyes can deceive you," the Jedi explains, "Don't trust them."

Perceptions form in our mind as images or ideas of things that we experience through sight, sound, taste, touch, smell, and thought. When someone says "Darth Vader" or "terrorist," for instance, we have specific images that form in our mind. These images may be entirely incongruous with reality, but they fashion the basis of our beliefs and actions. When we act on faulty perceptions we can cause harm to others and to ourselves.

Obi-Wan advises Luke not to trust his eyes because they are susceptible to deception. The same is true with our perceptions.

Without Obi-Wan's deep perception of emptiness we are deceived by our false ideas, and that can lead us down the dark path of suffering. Leia suffers because she believes Han is gone, but truly he has never left her—nor could he! Han remains ever in her heart—and in the *Millennium Falcon,* Chewbacca, and even in the traitorous Lando Calrissian.

This truth can be very difficult to grasp. Clearly Han *is* gone: there he is encased in a living coffin, and destined for Jabba's palace and an uncertain fate—anyone can see that! But when we hear Obi-Wan's words, "Your eyes can deceive you. Don't trust them," we remember to look deeper into life.

A great deal of our suffering, worries, and difficulties comes from our inability to see the truth of things. That means that although we see the *appearance* of something we often fail to recognize the deeper truths of its interdependent and interpenetrating nature. Han cannot be found solely in his body. We are conditioned by our ignorance to recognize Han only in the aggregate "form" and to view that form as having a separate, permanent existence. But that is just an idea, a false perception, because Han is by nature empty.

Although this may seem counterintuitive consider this: Does a rainbow have a separate, permanent existence? Can it exist in a vacuum? Is *it* a false idea, an illusion? When we see a rainbow, perhaps arching over a waterfall outside Theed, we distinguish it from the waterfall, the sky, and especially from ourselves. However, the rainbow only exists because of the interplay of interdependent conditions: the presence of air, water vapor in the air, sunlight hitting the vapor, and our personal perspective and perception. Each of these factors is impermanent, yet *each is necessary for there to be a rainbow.* And beyond these conditions and their interplay, there is no unchanging, separate, independent "self" that we can say *is by itself* the rainbow—and yet rainbows clearly *do* exist.

Like the rainbow, Han Solo is also made up of factors. We call them the five aggregates, and through their interplay that smug space pirate we all love comes into existence. And yet, beyond the five aggregates and their interplay, there is no unchanging, separate, independent "self" that we can say *is by itself* Han Solo—nonetheless Han does exist.

Misperception can create problems for us that are not so obscure as failing to see Han's presence in Lando or the *Millennium Falcon*. Luke's battle with himself in the dark side cave is caused by misperception. Or, to take myself as an example: If I were to overhear my friend talking in whispers to my wife I might, in my worst moments, become jealous and suspicious. I could imagine even thinking something un-Jedi-like and accuse my friend of trying to steal her away. But in fact, the two may have really been planning a surprise birthday party for me! If I were not careful about examining my perceptions they may cause a great rift in my relationship with both my friend and my wife.

QUI-GON INSTRUCTS OBI-WAN in *The Phantom Menace* to "be mindful of the living Force." For us to begin to undo the deception caused by misperceptions it is important to hone our mindfulness and concentration as Qui-Gon instructs. We can interpret Qui-Gon's directive in this way: *Be mindful of life in every moment, with every action.* So, to practice "living Force" mindfulness means when we brush our teeth, do a task at work or school, or dial the phone we do so *each time* with our *full awareness* as

though it were the first time we had ever done such a thing. We treat each moment with attention and respect even if we are doing something we have done a thousand times before or something we might not necessarily choose to do. This is a practice designed to help us not take anything for granted, to be in contact with "the living Force" of life at this moment, and to not be fooled by our misperceptions.

Our actions are often based on our preconceptions of people and things. Acting from this deceived perspective means we are not interacting with the real person or thing in question, we are relating with an *idea* of them, a perception. "Living Force mindfulness" cuts through perception and engages people as they truly are at this moment. For example, you see Darth Vader and the preconceptions you have of him form the basis of your actions and attitude toward him. You have seen him kill people, torture people, and be pretty much an all-around bad guy. And therefore you think you *know* Darth Vader—but you fail to see the man in front of you now is not the same person from yesterday. Our preconceptions prevent us from seeing a man who would sacrifice himself to save the son he had been trying to kill just ten minutes prior.

When we give our full attention to each moment our mind is prepared for anything and it is open to everything. Conversely, when we fail to be attentive or when think we already know someone we close ourselves off to that moment and that person, and miss the opportunity to experience them fully moment after moment.

In *The Empire Strikes Back* Luke's mind did not have the sort of clarity one experiences with "living Force mindfulness" and was subject to the deceptions of his erroneous perceptions. On

Dagobah, Luke believes that "size matters." Moving small stones around with the Force, he thinks, is entirely different from lifting his submerged X-wing. Unlike Luke's mind, the mind that treats each moment with freshness and awareness accepts things as they are in the present. Such a mind is not dualistic, dividing things into *this* and *that,* big and small, heavy and light—it understands differences but transcends discrimination and is unfettered by misperception. It is a mind in which "size matters not."

Recall that scene: Luke stands dejected at the edge of the swamp on Dagobah where only a small portion of his X-wing can be seen poking out of the murky water.

"Oh, no. We'll never get it out now," moans the crestfallen Jedi pupil.

Yoda, who has been calmly observing the situation, replies, "So certain are you. Always with you it cannot be done. Hear you nothing that I say?"

"Master, moving stones around is one thing. This is totally different."

"No! No different!" Yoda says. "Only different in your mind. You must unlearn what you have learned."

As children our minds are relatively free of erroneous divisions and preconceptions. We experience each thing, each event with wonder and originality, and often with direct mindfulness. The youthful mind has not yet learned to categorize things, people, and feelings into familiar packages of preconceptions. As a result a childlike mind is often able to touch life in ways that the older, more structured mind cannot.

Take Obi-Wan Kenobi's experience in *Attack of the Clones,* for example. Obi-Wan is unable to locate the planet Kamino in the Jedi Archives. Confounded, he approaches Yoda for assistance as the tiny Jedi Master is training a group of young Jedi. Upon presenting his dilemma to the group, a solution to Obi-Wan's problem becomes apparent: the planet had been erased from the Archive memory! It was not the older, more experienced Jedi that hit upon the solution, but a child—the Padawan J. K. Burtola. The child's mind, unlike Obi-Wan's, was less clouded by rigid facts, preconceptions, and set beliefs and could more readily see the truth. That is the advantage of "living Force mindfulness."

Perceptions often obfuscate our understanding of reality and give us an impression that is entirely wrong. Luke was wrong to think the rock and the X-wing were different. Yoda clearly demonstrated their nondualistic nature when he smoothly lifted the spacecraft out of the swamp. If Luke had been able to "unlearn" the rigid structure of his mind he would have seen the rock in the X-wing and the X-wing in the rock. He would have guided the ship out of the water as his master had.

The reality of interdependence and interpenetration surpasses all concepts. When we practice as Qui-Gon instructs, our mindfulness sweeps away misperceptions to reveal clear insight and understanding.

ANAKIN SKYWALKER'S BELIEF that he needs to be the most powerful Jedi ever initiates his movement toward the dark side and later shapes his character as Darth Vader, and this belief is an example the fourth component of the human being as the aggregate of *mental formations*. A *mental formation* is an idea or attitude that initiates action or directs and shapes one's character.

Mental formations can be present all the time, like attention, contact, or volition; or they can arise in specific circumstances, like determination, mindfulness, sleepiness.

Mental formations can sometimes be beneficial and sometimes harmful or neutral. Thinking is a mental formation that can be beneficial when our mind is clear and calm. At such times thinking helps us understand things better. But at other times, thinking can be unhelpful if our mind is scattered or shrouded by misperceptions.

Some mental formations can lead us to the dark side. Greed, ignorance, hatred, pride can initiate action that does not support our deepest happiness. The mental formations of ignorance, pride, and anger were likely driving Anakin's desire to be the most powerful Jedi ever.

With living Force mindfulness we can be aware of our mental formations as they arise in our mind. We recognize malice when it is present. We don't try to get rid of malice; we simply see our mind is, in this moment, full of malice. Recognizing malice with living Force mindfulness prevents malice from bullying us into actions that are harmful to ourselves and others.

Mental formations are the product of our upbringing, education, environment, and experiences. Anakin's life as a slave, his incomplete Jedi education, the Clone Wars were all necessary components that came together to form the mental formation that drove him to the dark side. Nowhere in a mental formation can one find a permanent, separate "self" that exists and functions outside of the interrelated web of all things.

THE FINAL AGGREGATE of the human being is *consciousness*. We will explore more about consciousness in chapter VI of this book. For the time being, however, it is sufficient to know that, like feelings, perceptions, and mental formations, consciousness is directly influenced by contact with the world of things and experiences, sometimes called the *world of phenomena*. As sense organs (the eye, the ear, and so on) come in contact with something, this triggers a seed deep in our consciousness creating a mental formation in our mind.

Consciousness is therefore a response to contact between, for example, your eyes and these words. As you read you are conscious of the printed words. When you hear the ominous breathing of Darth Vader you become conscious of his respiration (and no doubt fearful that some great evil is about to befall you). When you smell something noxious during your escape from cellblock AA23 you are conscious of the foul stench emanating from the Death Star trash compactor. As you run your hand along the S-foil of an X-wing you are conscious of its tactile smoothness broken intermittently by nicks and scores from countless battles against the Empire. When a spoonful of Yoda's dinner touches your tongue, you are instantly conscious of its unpalatable taste. Consciousness is always consciousness of something.

In many philosophies and religions "consciousness" carries the connotation of a separate, permanent self, or a soul—but not so in Buddhism. Consciousness arises out of *conditions*. Your eyes are a condition and these words are conditions that together produce eye-consciousness. The conditions of your ears and the phone ringing produce sound-consciousness. Consciousness is thus impermanent, changing with each interaction between the eye and form, the ear and sound, the tongue and taste, the body and tangible objects, and the mind and ideas.

Consciousness relies upon the world as much as it relies upon the mind and body. And because of this, consciousness changes from moment to moment. Nowhere in consciousness can one find an unchanging, separate, independent "self"—something that *is* us.

NOW LET US LOOK DEEPLY AT LEIA. Looking deeply

we see that she is made of five aggregates. All five are impermanent, and all five are a part of the world, continuously interacting with it. It is also important to see that each aggregate depends on and interpenetrates the other four. In *Return of the Jedi* Luke tells Leia that Darth Vader is his father. Luke's words meet Leia's ears producing sound-consciousness. From that consciousness, Leia's mind first forms a perception of Darth Vader. This is an image of a murderer and a creature of the dark side. Because she holds this perception her mind then fashions the mental formation of disgust (for Vader) and worry (for Luke). Disgust and worry produce bodily sensations (perhaps increased heart rate and muscle tension). Muscle tension and a rapid heart rate can be judged unpleasant feelings. From this elementary example we see that the five aggregates do not exist separately, but penetrate each other in a continuous flow of influence and counterinfluence.

With all this said, given that Leia is empty and made up of five aggregates that are themselves made up of everything else, can we say that Leia is real, that she is *really* here? The answer is yes—of course she is. Leia is here as the ex-senator, rebel-commanding, Han-loving daughter of the most feared man in the galaxy. She is also here as a manifestation of all that is, of all of life. This means that, while from one perspective she is a human being with a limited lifespan, she is also an aggregate of life itself—interdependent and continuously changing with the flow of life, limitless and free from notions of birth and death.

We are not permanent. Our body, feelings, perceptions, mental formations, and consciousness are never the same from one moment to the next. We are not independent. Each of the five aggregates penetrates, and is penetrated by, all of life. The body is born from the air, food, and water it receives. The body dies through the process of urination, defecation, and skin exfoliation leaving cells in the earth, air, and water. Feelings, perceptions, mental formations, and consciousness are born and die with the instant-to-instant interaction between the sense organs and the world of things and experience. And since a human being is made up entirely of form, feelings, perceptions, mental formations, and consciousness, we too are born and die with the instant-to-instant interaction between the sense organs and the world of things and experience.

In the next chapter we will see how attachment to the idea that we are a separate, permanent self is a cause of suffering, in ourselves and in Anakin Skywalker.

V ESCAPING TATOOINE

AND THE CAUSE OF SUFFERING

*"Are you allowed to love?
I thought that was forbidden for a Jedi."*

*"Attachment is forbidden…
Compassion, which I would define as unconditional love,
is central to a Jedi's life.
So you might say that we are encouraged to love."*

PADMÉ AMIDALA AND ANAKIN SKYWALKER
IN "ATTACK OF THE CLONES"

I N "ATTACK OF THE CLONES" Anakin Skywalker tells of his slaughter of Tusken Raiders: "I killed them. I killed them all. They're dead—every single one of them. And not just the men, but the women and the children too. They're like animals and I slaughtered them like animals. I hate them!"

We can almost feel Anakin's pain. His suffering is so deep and powerful that it's like a force of nature. But how does it come to be? Does the death of his mother alone give rise to such intense hate? Or is the cause something else, something more, something that took place in his own mind?

Suffering in our lives has a cause. That cause is the action of grasping or rejecting various forms of desire and ideas as they arise in our mind. Desires and ideas (or mental formations like Anakin's hatred) are themselves not suffering, and they should not be seen as a threat. Suffering is not the feeling of fear, the desire for revenge, or the belief in the soul, it is *attachment* and *aversion* to those things—or any of a host of others. In other words, suffering is the inability to accept things as they are without grasping or turning away.

We can say that there are three types of desire that, when grasped or rejected, cause suffering. The three types are: *desire for sense pleasure* (things that are pleasant to experience), *desire for non-being* (the wish for something to not be the way it is), and *desire for becoming* (that is, the desire to have more or to be more). Desire for sense pleasure creates suffering because its demands for eternal fulfillment are continually frustrated by the impermanent, unsatisfactory nature of the world of phenomena.

The Buddha said, "All phenomena that are born, exist, and are subject to the influence of other phenomena; in other words, all phenomena that are *composite*, must abide by the law of impermanence and eventually cease to exist. They cannot exist eternally, without some day being destroyed. Everything we cherish and hold dear today, we will have to let go of and be separated from in the future." *Composite,* in this passage, means "composed of separate elements."

Artoo is a composite being: He is composed of separate elements. Not just gears and wires, but also the ice of Hoth, Wedge, and the Imperial fleet. A tree on Endor is also composed of separate elements: the rain, sunlight, soil, and Ewoks. As we've seen everything is interrelated, and therefore everything is a composite. Everything is made up of everything else—existing in a continuous cycle of transformation.

We have a tendency to cling to things that bring us joy or make us happy, hoping they will never leave us. A mother may not want to see her child leave to become a Jedi, a basketball player may dread the day he has to hang up his sneakers, a model may quake at the thought of her beauty fading. But the fact is all these things leave us. We cannot stop change anymore than we can stop, as Shmi Skywalker, Anakin's mother, says, "the suns from setting." All things are of the nature to pass away; we suffer when we do not release them.

When things that bring us joy are gone we are left feeling hollow, and we try to fill up this hollowness with new things: Star Wars video games, decadent food, alcohol, Star Tours trips to Naboo. While each new thing can be a small joy, none provide us with lasting relief from that hollow feeling. They are all impermanent, and the contentment they bring today is gone tomorrow.

Please understand it is not the video games or flights of fantasy that cause suffering (we can surely enjoy them while they're here!), it is our desire to fill up our internal hollowness that creates in us a repetitive pattern of grasping, attainment, loss, and frustration—and that is suffering. The Buddha taught, "Living beings, led by craving, rush about aimlessly like trapped rabbits. Caught in their desires they suffer over and over again." When we are led by our desires, rather than free to take them or leave them, we are caught in a cycle of obtaining and losing, pleasure and frustration—and we suffer over and over again.

True suffering originates in our mind; we create it through our own ignorance and confusion. We hold the firm belief that if we get to leave Tatooine and train as a Jedi, or if we get that new job or the woman or man of our dreams, *then* we will be happy. We believe that true happiness arises from the acquisition of things, the attainment of some goal. When we have perspective we realize that of course the new job is not *the whole* of our happiness, but when we are caught in a desire, it seems to consume our entire world and we become convinced we can't live without it—and that *blind conviction* is suffering.

There is nothing wrong with wanting to become a Jedi or seeking better employment. We can happily choose to pursue either course without attachment, but if we are convinced that we must have it or life will be miserable then, if we fail, life *will* be miserable and we will be frustrated and bitter. And if we succeed, and attachment is still strong in us, we will quickly discover that, while it's great to be a Jedi, wouldn't it be better to be on the Council? Then we'll be off chasing another goal that, *this time,* we assure ourselves, will *certainly* solve all our problems and give us our "happily ever after" life. Sure it will.

Composite phenomena are not the only things that are impermanent, desires are as well. If we take the time to watch our mind carefully we will see that what arises also ceases. For example, the desire for a candy bar as we stroll passed the concession stand toward our tenth viewing of *Attack of the Clones* is but a momentary impulse. We can either choose to act on that impulse or let it drift away. But when we constantly act on every impulse and desire that pops up in our mind we can become caught in a habit of chasing after things, and then we will find it very difficult to be calm and happy with what is. The hunger of desire can never be satisfied once and for all, and it does not allow us to enjoy the present moment. It calls for sex or candy when we are trying to take a math test. It nags at us to forsake our Jedi training and race to Cloud City even though doing so will put our life and the freedom of the galaxy at stake. It pulls us out of the present moment and away from happiness.

IN "A NEW HOPE" Luke Skywalker cannot accept living on Tatooine. He is bored and feels trapped there because Uncle Owen will not allow him to leave to join the Academy. He longs to escape the drudgery of that desolate place to find romance and adventure among the stars.

This is an example of the second type of desire that produces suffering when grasped: desire for non-being. "Non-being" is just another way of saying *aversion,* the act of turning away. Aversion is frustration with life in the here and now. It is the desire to be rid of a dissatisfying situation. It is an energy that does not accept life in the present moment.

Just as Luke does while living on Tatooine, many of us believe the grass is always greener on the other side of the fence, that Tatooine (or, specifically, this moment) is the source of all our problems and "if only" we could escape it everything would be okay. We look at our existence and think how pathetic and dissatisfying it is and we suffer. We hold a deep conviction that happiness is not available to us in the here and now. We look to the future or to another place to find it and disregard the present moment and the present place.

In *The Phantom Menace* Qui-Gon Jinn informs young Anakin Skywalker, "Your focus determines your reality." Focusing on all the things we find unpleasant will create a reality that is unbearable. Life would become miserable, and we would be blind to all the beauty and joy present in it. Good health, food, education, shelter, and loved ones are available to us right now. If we ignore them because we think our life will be better somewhere else or in the hereafter we are bound to suffer right here, right now.

Yoda reproaches Luke in *The Empire Strikes Back* because his mind was never focused "on where he was, what he was doing," but lost in dreams of adventure and excitement. "A Jedi craves not these things," Yoda says. Craving is fine. It is when a Jedi *attaches* to craving that he suffers. And this will happen if the Jedi is not practicing living Force mindfulness. When we are doing this, when we are mindful of our cravings, we can *chose* to act on them if we think they will benefit us, rather than be a slave to them and *obey* them whenever they make a noise.

ANAKIN SKYWALKER LOSES HIMSELF in his desire

to be the most powerful Jedi ever. The good man that was Anakin is destroyed, and he becomes Darth Vader. This is an example of the third type of desire—*becoming*. Becoming is the near opposite of aversion: aversion is the desire to be rid of something; becoming is the almost blind quest to attain it.

Craving to be famous, to have authority, to be like Yoda are examples of this third type of desire. When we pursue ideas of becoming we lose the peace right here and right now. Buddhist practice, like Jedi training, is a path of self-awareness. The arts of mindfulness and concentration, and meditation too, are intended to help us get in touch with who we are. They are not designed to turn us into someone else. We cannot become anything more than what we already are.

Attachment to the idea of becoming "the most powerful Jedi ever" or an "enlightened being" is a quick road to frustration and unhappiness. The key is not *becoming*, but rather *understanding*. The more we understand ourselves the less we will suffer by clinging to the idea that we need to get rid of who we are and become just like a little green Jedi Master.

The two forms of desire just mentioned, becoming and aversion, arise when the mind is critical, judgmental, and ignorant. They manifest as a voice in our head saying, "This place sucks," or "I shouldn't be such a coward," or (with very serious conviction) "I hate Jar Jar so much I wish Anakin would rip out his tongue and shove it down his incessantly jabbering mouth!" In such a state of mind we can never be good enough, and life can never be good enough. Grasping hold of these thoughts, these forms of desire, is suffering and it can cause us to do and say things that we might regret.

But we do not need to be a slave to the critical mind. We can observe it and simply reflect, "Right now my mind is critical." This does not mean we try to *get rid of* our critical mind. We just become aware of it and follow our breathing so that we stay anchored and are not swept away by the negative thoughts. In just a brief amount of time we will discover that the critical thoughts have drifted away. They are impermanent phenomena. We do not need to chase them away, attach to them or analyze them. Just observe.

CONSIDER THIS SCENE IN *Attack of the Clones:*

Anakin has accompanied Padmé to an audience with the new queen of Naboo. The topic of Padmé's protection is broached, and Sio Bibble, the governor of Naboo, asks Anakin, "What is your suggestion, Master Jedi?"

"Oh, Anakin's not a Jedi yet." Padmé answers for him, "He's still a Padawan Learner. But I was thinking…"

Anakin, his ego bruised, interrupts, "Hold on a minute…."

Before he can continue, Padmé, who was sensitive to political decorum, silences him and continues with her conference only to be interrupted once again by a now resentful Anakin. "Excuse me!" he says. "I'm in charge of security here, m'lady."

In this scene, Anakin is attempting to "save face" and maintain his position, but, drunk on pomposity, ends up behaving the fool. Padmé doesn't hesitate to point this out to him and set him in his place. Before the queen, the governor, and other dignitaries,

Anakin is forced to swallow his pride. With outright sullenness and a face that is quintessential indignation he grudgingly relents and mutters behind clenched teeth, "Sorry, m'lady."

In this scene, Anakin grasps onto the belief he has been shown disrespect, perhaps even disparaged, and his sense of self flares up in anger. The feelings of anger, indignation, pride, and sullenness are subtle forms of suffering and are the result, in this instance, of Anakin's firm attachment to the false view of the self or the ego.

The false view of self is a pervasive source of suffering and one that is not easily released. However, it is important to remember that it is just an idea, an impermanent belief, which *can* be released.

Attachment to the notion that the five aggregates of being are a separate, permanent self is not only a major source of suffering— it is also dangerous. It can produce selfishness, hatred, and arrogance that can lead to conflicts between friends, families, and even nations and worlds. It can also lead to internal struggles with the dark side that, in Darth Vader's case, have galactic repercussions.

But grasping onto our beliefs can also produce little sorrows in our daily life. Reflecting on how attached we are to the belief we are separate beings reveals a great deal of egotism and insecurity in us—as we saw in the above example with Anakin. When we watch our mind we see that it is constantly critiquing others, comparing ourselves to them, and jostling for respect. One moment we feel we are better than those around us, the next we feel we are worse than them.

Attachment to ideas can also lead to the dark side of suffering in ways that are not plainly linked to the false view of self. To again take myself as an example: in my life I have developed certain beliefs about the way things are or the way things should be done.

For instance, whenever I had a paper due for a class I would take a few days or a week or two to immerse myself in it. My life would become the paper as I forgot about shaving, basic hygiene, and often eating so I could complete the assignment. The idea I had grasped hold of was that I would be happier just to be done with the paper. So I would generally make myself miserable for a given span of time so that I could be "free" of the paper. This was not a wise course of action because I was never really happy. I was not happy when I was working on the paper, and when it was done I was simply too delirious and exhausted to enjoy its completion.

Despite recognizing that this method was less than satisfying, I continued to employ it throughout my college career because I was attached to the idea that it was a good approach. We all have many similar attachments. We firmly believe that things must be done "this way." We cling to beliefs about the "proper" way to box our comics (with backboards!), or the "only" way to watch the Star Wars DVDs (letterbox!), or which movie is the "best" Star Wars (*The Empire Strikes Back*!). These may seem like insignificant forms of attachment, but any time we are stuck in a rut of thinking, we are limiting our range of happiness. Practicing living Force mindfulness reveals these areas of attachment and when we see them we can let them go and do them freely and without attachment. Then taking the time to cook a healthy meal (even in the midst of writing a term paper) will not seem like such a major waste of time.

IN "ATTACK OF THE CLONES" Anakin Skywalker reveals

yet another form attachment that causes suffering—attachment to infatuated romantic love or the desire to "possess" another. Consider this scene:

Aboard a transport en route to Naboo, Padmé remarks to Anakin that it must be hard for him to have sworn his life to the Jedi. Anakin replies that it is indeed difficult because he cannot be with the people he loves.

"Are you allowed to love?" Padmé asks. "I thought that was forbidden for a Jedi."

Anakin responds wryly, "Attachment is forbidden... Compassion, which I would define as unconditional love, is central to a Jedi's life. So you might say that we are encouraged to love."

Anakin seems to have turned the entire concept of unconditional love and attachment upside-down. First, it is not wise to *forbid* attachment because if we think, "I should not be attached to this or that desire," we are pushing away that desire, we are trying to suppress it, and that then becomes a cause of suffering. Pushing away is not something a wise Jedi would do. Attaching to a desire leads to the suffering of becoming. Pushing away desire leads to the suffering of aversion. Instead, when a desire arises in our mind it is wise to practice living Force mindfulness and simply observe it. We do not grasp it, but at the same time we do not turn from it. We just watch it in mindfulness and accept it. It is just a desire, and it is our choice what to do about it. Our choice can lead to freedom and joy, but it can also lead to suffering. Anakin's second error (and one that Padmé seems to share) centers on his confusion over the meanings of *unconditional* and *romantic* love. He defines compassion as unconditional love. This seems right however, the remainder of Anakin's speech is just word games. Anakin suggests that unconditional love is the same as romantic love, and therefore he is "encouraged" to pursue Padmé. Unconditional love, by definition, means love "without conditions"—love without attachment. This is love for the sake of loving—love that is not bound to any one person or thing, and not dependent on being required in any way. Romantic love is infatuation for a particular person and is often wrapped up with selfish desires and needs that have nothing really to do with the person we believe we love.

In reality, the type of love Anakin describes when he argues that he was encouraged to love was not unconditional love, it was romantic love. Romantic love is not the love of Obi-Wan's insight into the symbiont cycle of life. Romantic love is attached, infatuated love. In attached love, the lover thinks he cannot express love unless it is to a particular individual. In other words, Anakin's love is *conditioned* or *dependent on* loving only Padmé, or at least his *idea* of Padmé. This is not the unconditional love of compassion, which is love regardless of the person or thing. Infatuated love is love that is doled out only when the object of one's love fulfills specific needs or demands, demands that are usually unconscious or unspoken. This means when our loved ones fail to meet our needs we leave them or "fall out of love" with them. This is not to say that romantic love is a bad thing, but it is not unconditional love and if we reflect on it we see that infatuated romantic love produces suffering.

Anakin suffers when Padmé is not near him—and he suffers when she *is* near him. He says longingly, "From the moment I met you…not a day has gone by when I haven't thought of you." This is suffering due to separation from what we are attached to. He continues, "And now that I'm with you again, I'm in agony. The closer I get to you the worse it gets." In the book version of *Attack of the Clones,* Anakin goes on to say, "The thought of not being with you makes my stomach turn over, my mouth go dry…I can't breathe!" So, even when he is with his beloved, Anakin suffers because he fears he will one day be without her.

Anakin is attached to the idea that being with Padmé equals eternal happiness. Many of us believe, perhaps on some unconscious level, some version of this same thing. We are convinced that attainment of this person will make us happy forever. But if we do not take care to observe desire and learn to move forward in our relationship with our eyes open to the fact that it cannot bring us true freedom and happiness, we will be pulled into a cycle of desire, attainment, and suffering.

Romantic love can also be a source of suffering because it is often based on misperceptions about the object of our love. We can invest so much of our hopes and dreams into one person that we build a monument to them in our mind and thus fail to see that they are just human beings. Anakin does this the first time he meets Padmé in *The Phantom Menace* when he compares her to an angel. *Apotheosis,* exalting glorification, can cause discontent in our life because no one can ever meet the superhuman qualities we have attributed to them in our minds. Our loved ones are after all human—they are imperfect, ever changing, and can never completely give us true happiness. Placing our expectations for eternal happiness on them is not true love, and it is not something a wise Jedi would do.

I believe most of us can relate to Anakin. I know I can. I am certainly capable of placing my hopes for happiness and love on another person. I know that I am attached to my wife, and I often think I cannot be happy without her. This is only natural when one does not see reality clearly, but in those few precious moments when I do see things as they truly are, my fear of being without her lifts off me. But this does not mean I dispense with her or stop loving her. On the contrary, my love for her grows and transcends the paltry limits of romance and neediness. And her presence in my life becomes that much more genuinely cherished.

Unconditional love, as opposed to romantic love, does *not* produce suffering because it is not attached to anything; it has no expectations and no restrictions. Unconditional love accepts the impermanent nature of its loved one. It understands that people change, and it adjusts to those changes without selfish demands or pressures. This does not mean that we are milksops when a loved one turns abusive or harms us in some way. If conditions arise that require us to break off a friendship or end a marriage, then unconditional love gives us the wisdom and strength to do so without closing our heart to the person who has hurt us. When some one hurts us we know that it is because they suffer.

Unconditional love is also free to love *every being* and is not fixed to one particular person as the sole object of its kindness. Unconditional love is a *practice* and, although it sounds nice to speak of it, it is not something we can decide to do perfectly from this moment forward. The arts of mindfulness and concentration, meditation and deep looking help us clear away the walls our minds have created between ourselves and others. When these walls are down love, unconditional and undemanding, rushes in to fill their place.

THE BUDDHA TAUGHT that the awakened person does not feel repugnance for the ugly nor attachment to the beautiful, but realizes that all things are impermanent and exist in a state of confluence with one another. And yet so often we truly believe that we cannot live happily without certain people, certain situations, certain things. We are convinced that life is unbearable where we are so we must go somewhere else, be with someone else, or do something new. But if we act on this belief, if we grasp superfluous desires, do we ever really find freedom and true happiness? This is something each of us must ask ourselves deeply and often.

IN "THE EMPIRE STRIKES BACK" Yoda admonishes Luke because he seems to want adventure and excitement: "A Jedi craves not these things." This is not exactly sound advice because it suggests that one should *get rid* of craving. In reality, however, it is important that we accept craving and wrap it with our mindfulness. If we try to push it away because we want to be "above" it then we will just be attaching to another form of desire, the desire of non-being, or aversion. Instead we allow desire to just be—like a cloud floating across the sky of our mind.

Allowing the desire to be means we accept it. We notice that greed, for instance, is present in our mind, and we think, "This is greed." We accept greed as greed. We do not identify with greed, get down on ourselves and think, "Oh look, I am being greedy again. I am such a greedy person." To identify with the greed means we are grasping greed. We are saying, "I *am* greed." This is a wrong view and causes suffering. Greed is just greed. It is a mental formation that comes into being when things are right for it; it has no bearing on our worthiness.

If we can accept desire when it arises and watch it we will see that it ceases. It is sometimes difficult to remember that desire is impermanent. If we have a particularly relentless desire we might think it will nag us until we give in, and so we do give in just to quiet it.

Imagine you have a persistent desire to tell off your boss or your teacher. When you grasp it and yell at her you may feel satisfied. But this satisfaction is just a temporary reprieve; it is not freedom from the desire (and it could potentially get you fired—killed if your boss happens to be a Sith Lord!). To be free of the desire you need to learn to leave it alone and allow it to cease naturally—that is true freedom.

The practice of recognizing, accepting, and allowing desire to be is how we let go of desire. It is simply dwelling stably with the desire, watching it without reacting. This is an active choice, the act of letting go, and when we release the desire to do something unwholesome we experience a wonderful feeling, but this does not mean the desire is gone forever. It is only gone *for the moment.* However, the more the habit of letting go replaces that of attachment the more freedom we enjoy.

YODA eloquently displays letting go in *Return of the Jedi:* He has seen the galaxy fall from peace into chaos. He has witnessed the Sith take over and the Jedi all but disappear. He knows his life is ending and the dark side still holds sway over the galaxy. Yet he does not suffer from aversion to that new order. He does not suffer by desperately clinging to his ideas, his beliefs, or the five aggregates of self. He knows twilight is upon him and night will soon fall. He is able to let go and accept that whatever is subject to arising is subject to ceasing. "That is the way of things," he says, "the way of the Force."

In the next chapter we will examine ways to take care of our suffering so we may better accept, like Master Yoda, "the way of the Force."

VI KNOWING THE GOOD SIDE

FROM THE DARK SIDE

"But how am I to know the good side from the bad?"

"You will know. When you are calm, at peace. Passive."

LUKE SKYWALKER AND MASTER YODA
IN "THE EMPIRE STRIKES BACK"

Hard to see the Dark Side is."

This is Master Yoda's response to Qui-Gon Jinn's assertion that the Sith had surfaced once again. Ten years later when civil war threatens to engulf the Galactic Republic the dark side has become very *easy* to see. In fact, for Master Yoda it is difficult to see anything else because the dark side has clouded everything.

Much like the dark side, the source of our suffering is often hard to see, especially our role in causing it. Our fear and shame of suffering often obscures our ability to face it and see its true roots, and our anger at the fact of suffering may obscure our vision still further. Left uncared for, suffering can grow and grow until it becomes like the dark side in *Attack of the Clones*—a gloomy shroud that hangs over everything. That's why it is important to take care of our suffering now before it can overwhelm us.

Mindfulness and meditative contemplation can clear away the storm clouds of suffering, ease mind and body, and bring understanding. Understanding helps us care for suffering so we do not pass it on to others as Anakin did when his suffering overwhelmed him and he massacred every man, woman, and child in the Tusken camp. If you pay attention you will notice that every time you are angry or sad your friends and family suffer. Their suffering may be sorrow, or it may be resentment, but whatever it is your state of mind affects them. Taking care of your suffering means you are also taking care of your friends and family. Taking care of suffering is a deeply loving act.

Taking care of suffering means we practice like the Jedi and pay attention to what we are doing right now. We cultivate mindfulness so that we can be aware of our emotions and how they interact with the world. Doing this helps us gain insight into the conditions that give rise to suffering. These conditions can be misperceptions, desires, or even world events. Numerous conditions join together to produce suffering, and recognizing them can free us from a lot of our unhappiness.

THE CONDITIONS that give rise to suffering (or happiness) are known as *nutriments*. Looking into anything that exists one could find the nutriments that have helped it come to be and continue to feed it. There are four kinds of nutriments that feed us: edible food, sense impressions, intention, and consciousness. The first nutriment is *edible food.* Food, drink, and other things we consume orally have an effect on our physical, emotional, and mental well-being. Eating a lot of fatty foods that are high in cholesterol can lead to physical unpleasantness such as a heart attack. Consuming quantities of alcohol can destroy our liver. Smoking makes cancer a greater threat. These physical calamities clearly have an impact on our emotional happiness. When we are sick we can become irritable or, in the case of life-threatening diseases, deathly afraid. Some things that we consume—like Episode II's "death sticks"—can do great harm to our mind. Illicit drugs can rob us of our memory, our ability to think abstractly, and even our life.

Mindful eating is a way to avoid the pitfalls associated with the first nutriment. Mindful eating does not just mean awareness of the physical act of chewing and swallowing, it also means being conscious of *what* we are eating, where it has come from, and how it will affect our mind and body, and the world. If we find that we are usually tired and worn down we may want to look at our diet. Foods high in sugar and lacking necessary vitamins and minerals can produce lethargy. If waking up in the morning is extremely difficult with our head pounding like it always does, then it might be wise to drink fewer beers the night before. If picking up our infant niece seems as difficult as lifting an X-wing, we may want to cut back on the cigarettes.

Our eyes allow us to see the vast dunes of Tatooine, the astonishing waterfalls of Naboo, and the rebel assault on the Death Star. Our ears bring us the joy of hearing John Williams's music, the electric hum of the lightsaber, and the jarring twang of seismic charges. Through our body we experience life. Yet the more we ingest things that are unhealthy and the more we damage mind and body, the less opportunity will we have to deeply touch life with joy and freedom. When we take good care of our body by eating mindfully we protect ourselves from physical ailments and discomforts that keep us from enjoying in the present moment.

WE HEAR OBI-WAN AND ANAKIN ARGUE,

we feel the cool breeze blowing across the lake near Padmé's home district, we taste Aunt Beru's blue milk, we see Darth Maul battle Qui-Gon, and we smell the funeral pyre lit for Darth Vader. These are examples of the second nutriment, *sense impression*. Sense impression is the contact of our sense organs with the world around us. For the Buddhist, as for the Jedi, there are six sense organs—the eyes, ears, nose, tongue, body, and mind. These six are in continual contact with the world. Through our senses we take in countless "foods" that give rise to thoughts and perceptions in our mind based on the contact of our sense organs with the objects of their impression.

We can imagine, as did the Buddha, sensory food as millions of little bugs swarming over a diseased cow. The cow suffers from a disease that has wracked its skin, leaving its body exposed to the elements. Wherever the cow goes the insects come to suck on its blood and burrow into its flesh. We are like that cow—and the worldly phenomena we encounter are like those bugs. Wherever we go we are receiving millions of sensory inputs from the world. The arguments we hear, breeze we feel, taste of our food, smell of a fire, and violence we witness are the sensory inputs that we consume. And we are eating continuously. Billboards, commercials, and other advertisements encourage us to buy products that will seemingly make our life better. Magazines and movies show us how we should look, dress, and behave. Conversations we overhear, or participate in, form our opinions about world events. Some sensory inputs produce happiness and ease (contact with the good side of the Force), while others produce discomfort and suffering (contact with the dark side of the Force).

"BUT HOW AM I TO KNOW THE GOOD SIDE

from the bad?" Luke asks in *The Empire Strikes Back*. To which Yoda responds, "You will know. When you are calm, at peace. Passive." With these words, Yoda describes a state of calm reflection, a method by which we will be able to watch our sensory consumption and see how it alters our mood.

Seeing Anakin and Padmé kiss in *Attack of the Clones* might stimulate romantic cravings. Hearing Chewbacca's howl of despair as his best friend is frozen in carbonite might evoke sorrow in us. Some sensory food may create agitation or even anger in us. We may find that when we arrive at work or school we are often in a foul mood. If we look at the sensory food we consume before we reach that place we may begin to understand the source of our hostility. We find that on our way to work we tend to listen to a contentious radio talk-show host who revels in corrosive speech. Every morning we eat the host's toxic words and later it eats us. We arrive at work in a mood as venomous as the host's words. Mindfulness and self-observation will reveal the sensory foods that bring us happiness and those that bring us "dis-ease."

It is important that we observe our sensory food "passively"— as Yoda advises. When we are passive in the sense Yoda means it we are less likely to become hostile in the face of hostility. We merely observe. "The talk-show host's words are hostile. His words invoke hostility in me. Hostility is an unpleasant feeling. I will let it pass." When we observe our sensory food in this way we see it simply as hostility, or kindness, or any number of things. We do not label it as morally good or bad. Rather, we label it according to the feelings it produces in us. Does it create ease and happiness or does it make us feel agitated and miserable?

In our world of continual spin, sound bites, and pop-up banners it is vital that we remain aware of our sensory diet. If we are not careful about the sensory toxins we are consuming they will consume us.

IN "ATTACK OF THE CLONES" Anakin Skywalker states his intention to become the most powerful Jedi ever. Anakin believes that if he could become omnipotent he would be happy and make the galaxy a better place. He wants power in order to bring peace, to help people, and even to "learn to stop people from dying." This is an example of the third nutriment, our *intention*—our desire to obtain something, do something, achieve something, be something. Anakin did not intend to be a murderer and a villain, but because he becomes blinded by the shroud of the dark side that is exactly what his intentions lead him to. He does not want to lose Padmé as he lost his mother. So he does what he feels he must do: he embraces the dark side.

We all want to be happy, but so often our ideas, worldview, and perceptions lead us away from happiness. The question we need to ask ourselves is, "Will my present course of action support my deepest happiness or work against it?" If we don't mindfully contemplate this question we may end up like Anakin—caught in the dark side of suffering. To avoid this tragedy we must practice the method of calm reflection taught by Yoda and look carefully at our intentions and the ideas we have about obtaining what we seek. If we don't, we may chase after imagined conditions of happiness that actually lead us away from true happiness, or we can become so riveted on a single beacon of happiness that we become blind to everything else. We may have happiness pounding on our door, but we do not open it because through the peephole it looks nothing like what we've been hoping for.

The dark side offers Anakin the power to keep his loved ones alive and to bring order to the galaxy—but he becomes caught in the idea of that power. He thinks that the power to control life and order things as he sees fit is the only way to have peace, and until he can have that he will not be happy. Becoming blind to everything else, Anakin embraces the dark side to "save" Padmé and later he condones horrible acts of oppression and murder in the name of galactic stability. But massacring rebels, blowing up Alderaan or trying to alter the natural course of life does not bring peace. Instead it brings suffering, both to him and to the galaxy of which he is an interdependent part. Although his intention was to find happiness and to help others, Anakin's mistaken ideas led him farther and farther away from happiness and generosity and deeper into the dark side.

The Buddha offered a parable to demonstrate how our intentions, once locked into the nav computer of our mind, can pull us irresistibly toward the precise coordinates of suffering: Two large, strong men drag another man across the ground toward a blazing fire. The captive cannot break free from the grasp of the larger men, and he is thrown into the fire. The strong men represent our intention pulling us uncontrollably toward unhappiness. We do not want to be tossed into the fire of suffering, but our intentions inexorably draw us there.

We get the things we wish for, the things we imagine will make us permanently happy, and yet that feeling of being happily complete is not there. The force of our intention carries us forward to something else, something new, something more, but never to where we want to go, never to true happiness.

Even the most noble, most respectable intention—the intention to transform suffering and offer love to the world—can cause grief. It can cause grief because our *idea* of what transforming suffering and offering love to the world is may be entirely wrong. That is why we reflect in the way Yoda taught and remain vigilantly mindful as

Qui-Gon instructed so that we do not get lost along the dark path of false ideas.

We can do this by practicing the way of non-attainment. Sitting in meditation one does not try to attain enlightenment or manifest insight, one simply breathes, concentrating fully on the process of breathing. Through meditative concentration and mindfulness comes insight and awakening. When we are able to cultivate these qualities in ourselves happiness and freedom will naturally arise and we will be able to offer true love to the world, not just an idea of it.

CONSCIOUSNESS is the next nutriment. According to Buddhist psychology, consciousness is divided into eight parts. The upper realm of consciousness contains mind consciousness plus the five senses of sight, hearing, taste, touch, and smell. *Manas,* the clinging nature of our mind, is the narrow layer of consciousness in the middle. And the foundational layer of consciousness is called *storehouse consciousness.* (See Figure 1).

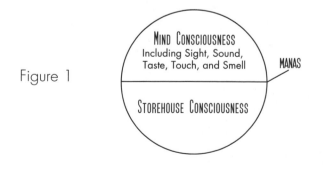

Figure 1

Storehouse consciousness has that name because it is a like a big warehouse storing every kind of seed. In our storehouse consciousness are seeds of hatred, joy, jealousy, lust, kindness—and everything else imaginable. We experience the various seeds when they blossom in our mind as a mental formation.

For example, when Luke sees his sister Leia after the fall of the second Death Star the seed of joy is clearly present in him. Luke is happy to see Leia. She is a living memory of Luke's parents, she is kind and supportive, and Luke loves her. The more Luke sees his sister the more the seed of joy will manifest in his mind consciousness. The longer the seed of joy is present in the mind's consciousness, the stronger it will become.

Every moment whether awake or asleep our consciousness is eating the world around us, including our own thoughts, feelings, and actions. Whatever we come in contact with our consciousness saves to release at another time—perhaps in a dream, or an ill-considered word. Many of these manifestations are subtle and fleeting. Others can be more persistent. For example, Anakin's experience as a slave, the Jedi Council's disapproval of his training, the so-called rigidity of his master, his "failure" to save his mother—all these may have watered the seeds of ambition in him. And ambition grew in him—ambition to rise above his status, ambition to stop his loved ones from dying, ambition to make others pay for hurting him. These ambitions, born from what he might see as the persistent suppression of his desires and of his hope for a better life, become part of his character and open him to the dark side. Because the nutriment of consciousness is subtle we need to be mindful of what we come in contact with, and which seeds are manifesting in our minds.

AS WE PAY ATTENTION to the seeds manifesting in our minds we may recognize the presence of unwholesome desires. Unwholesome means leading us away from true freedom. With Jedi-like mindfulness we watch these desires without disgust or attachment. Sometimes after just a few breaths the unwholesome desire is gone, and we are no longer enslaved by it. However, other times the desire persists. On these occasions "changing the peg" is a useful practice.

"Changing the peg" is a practice that may be employed when we are caught in unwholesome thoughts or desires. In the Buddha's time, and perhaps on such places as Endor, furniture was constructed with wooden pegs instead of metal nails or screws. Over time those pegs weakened and needed replacement. Carpenters hammered out the bad pegs and replaced them with good ones. We can do the same thing with our desires and unwholesome mental formations.

The craving for a cigarette, say, manifests as a seed in our mind consciousness. Recognizing it we try to hold it mindfully, breathing calmly to allow it to fade away—but it persists, clinging to our mind as the dianoga in the Death Star's trash compactor clung to Luke. The desire nags us, pushing us in a direction we do not wish to go.

In these times of difficulty we may focus our attention away from the desire to something else. We hammer out the "peg" of the desire for a cigarette and replace it with a different, more wholesome "peg"—such as honing our Jedi skills by running to the park or exercising in some other way, stepping out of our environment and enjoying the sunset, or putting on some music (perhaps an excellent John Williams score!). This may require all our concentration, but after awhile the craving will fade away. Each time we are able to disregard the demand of the craving it will lose power over us. Eventually it will hold no sway over us, and we will be free.

Changing the peg is an especially useful practice when our desires seem overwhelming or when we are caught in a deep trench of suffering that we cannot seem to find a way out of. If our mind is acutely critical of itself or if we are feeling depressed, rather than immersing ourselves in examination of our suffering and mulling it over in a continuous cycle of unhelpful thought, it is sometimes more useful for us to simply change the peg. This could mean we change our environment or we change the focus of our attention.

Changing our environment could be leaving our noisy apartment and taking a walk in the local park. Or we can turn off the noise of our negative or pestering thoughts and turn our attention to things that give rise to more nurturing thoughts. Often, when I am caught in a treadmill of damaging thought that is drawing the dark side around me like mynocks to a power coupling, I find it helpful to stop the stream of thought and look around. I see how lucky I am to be alive, to have seen the Star Wars films, to have friends and family that care for me and accept my geeky habit of dressing up like Star Wars characters. Life is really not that bad, and the things that I thought I needed…well, I'm really actually okay without them. Then the unwholesome desires or the negative thoughts that a moment ago seemed like the whole world fall into perspective, and their influence begins to drift away.

The lesson we can take from the practice of changing the peg is the importance of finding ways to nourish our joy and ease everyday. Practicing walking meditation in nature, playing in a lake or ocean, looking at inspirational works of art are ways we can nourish ourselves. Without a practice that waters seeds of happiness we will quickly dry up and become bitter, disillusioned people. This was the case, as we will shortly see, with Anakin Skywalker.

IN "THE EMPIRE STRIKES BACK" Yoda says, "A Jedi must have the deepest commitment, the most serious mind." To be aware of our consciousness, intentions, and the impact edible food and sense impressions have on us it is important to have the seriousness and commitment of a Jedi. This kind of determination is part of the practice of right effort, which may also be defined as any diligent action or thought that leads to spiritual freedom and happiness. If one hopes to transform one's suffering, then one needs to have "the deepest commitment" and "the most serious mind"—they are *required* for true happiness just as much as they are for being a Jedi.

At the same time, however, one must be cautious not to take the serious mind too far. Right effort does not entail a harsh meditation practice or straining oneself to attain some special state of mind, special insight, or special powers. If one practices in this way it will only make life more difficult and less enjoyable. Anakin Skywalker is a perfect example.

Anakin did not practice right effort or the kind of commitment Yoda says a Jedi must have. His intense desire to become more powerful and to do what he stubbornly feels is right set him on a path that allowed nothing short of perfection. In *Attack of the Clones,* Anakin imagines he should be all-powerful and beyond human emotions like anger. Because of his rigid attitude about what he should do and how powerful he should be he blames himself for his mother's death. Standing over her grave he says, "I wasn't strong enough to save you, mom…I won't fail again." His subsequent quest for strength and power, coupled with his non-acceptance of failure, eventually led him to the dark side where he suffered immensely as Darth Vader.

Many of us live, in some way, as Anakin did. We establish an impossible standard of perfection for ourselves that will not allow failure. But failure in the face of such imagined perfection is unavoidable. When we fail we feel unworthy, and we criticize ourselves for being no good or too stupid to do anything right. We sink into depression, guilt, or shame. Forcing ourselves to live under conditions of perfection does not make us better people, it does not help us do what is "right," it only brings us and everyone we encounter misery.

Right effort and deep commitment should not be harsh. They are a practice of ease and compassion. If our practice is a struggle because we are unable to meet the severe standards we have established for ourselves then we will abandon it, and that would be unfortunate. We must not punish ourselves for failing to be mindful or for being swept away by our emotions. A balance between accepting things as they are and working toward perfection has to be struck.

There is a Buddhist story that illustrates this:

The Buddha once called on a monk named Sona, who had been a musician, and asked him, "Sona, before you were ordained as a monk, were you clever at the lute's stringed music?"

"Yes, Lord," said Sona.

"When the strings of the lute were too taut, was it tuneful and fit for playing?"

"Certainly not, Lord," responded Sona.

"And when they were too slack, was the lute tuneful and fit for playing?"

"No, Lord."

The Buddha continued, "But when the strings were neither too taut or too slack, but keyed to an even pitch, was the lute tuneful and fit for playing?"

Sona replied, "Yes, Lord."

The same is true with our practice. The deep commitment of a Jedi is necessary, but our intensity should be tempered with ease. If it is not, the too taut string of our effort may snap.

Unfortunately too many of us think we need to treat ourselves like Darth Vader treats his officers in *The Empire Strikes Back*. When his officers fail, they are killed. When we fail the judgmental nature of our mind seeks to kill our shortcomings. This is a very imprudent course of action because failure is a wonderful aspect of life. Failure is what helps us learn, grow, and understand. From our failures we can see our nature more clearly, and from that we reap wisdom and understanding.

Anakin does not understand this. He incarcerates himself in a prison of perfection. Such a prison does not allow us to be human, to have shortcomings. It binds us to an idea that cannot be achieved. And when we are caught by this idea we are shackled to suffering. In the DVD-version of *Attack of the Clones* we see the enormity Anakin's suffering:

Anakin has just told Padmé about slaughtering the Tusken Raiders, who have kidnapped and tortured his mother. Through his sobs he tells her that although he knows better, he cannot stop from hating them. Padmé compassionately tells him that for killing his mother they earned his anger. "To be angry is to be human," she says, and wisely.

Anakin, however, cannot hear the deeper meaning of her words and says, "I'm a Jedi. I know I'm better than this."

This is an unfortunate but nonetheless common misunderstanding that many of us share with Anakin. We believe that to be better we have to control feelings like anger and jealousy, that having such feelings is a sign of weakness. We believe that it is not "Jedi" or "Buddhist" or "right" or "good" to be angry or jealous, so we repress it, deny it, or fight it. This is an unwise way to live.

By controlling hatred—in other words, denying it and separating ourselves from it—we miss the opportunity to take care of it and to transform it. If we are as wise as many of the Jedi seem to be we will not control our feelings but acknowledge, accept, and investigate them with mindfulness. With mindfulness and deep looking comes insight into the nature of our negative thoughts and feelings, and when we understand, we can release them and no longer be ruled by them.

It is also foolish to control our feelings, because when we attempt to do so we often end up repressing them. Repressing emotions only causes them to fester and later erupt like a volcano of suffering. Anger, for example, is like a cut on our finger. If we ignore it out of some sort of exaggerated stoicism it will only become infected, causing us increased sorrow and prolonging the healing process.

To control anger is also unwise because we *do* feel anger. We also feel joy, sorrow, and boredom. This is what it is to be human. We do not need to deny our humanity and strive to be indifferent automatons. We can accept who we are and give up the impossible quest to be perfect.

Anakin's idea of what a Jedi should be prohibits him from being fully human and so he ends up becoming a monster. To feel anger toward the people that tortured and murdered his mother is a natural human response. But Anakin finds this aspect of his humanity to be a weakness, and so, as Darth Vader, he learns to control his anger and unleash it as a deadly weapon.

Anakin also denies himself simple human failure. Kneeling over his mother's grave, Anakin promises her he will never fail again. No human could ever keep that promise; everyone at some time or other fails at something or in some way. With his promise not to fail again, Anakin seals his path to becoming "more machine than man." He discards his humanity, his emotions, his right to failure, and embraces the cold-hearted prison of perfection.

When we take care of suffering it has less of a hold on us and, in turn, less impact on those around us. Suffering is a realistic assessment of what it is to be human, but with Jedi-like commitment and compassionate practice we can begin to release our attachment to the causes of suffering, and this produces happiness. But it is up to us to do this. It is our actions in body, speech, and mind that lead us down the dark path or toward the good side. This is called *karma*, and it is the subject of our next chapter.

DARTH VADER'S KARMA

"Remember, a Jedi can feel the Force flowing through him."

"You mean it controls your actions?"

"Partially. But it also obeys your commands."

OBI-WAN KENOBI AND LUKE SKYWALKER
IN "A NEW HOPE"

I N "RETURN OF THE JEDI" Darth Vader makes a decision that changes everything. He chooses to forsake his loyalty to the dark side and to destroy his evil master, Emperor Palpatine, thereby saving his son even as he brings about his own death. Yet Vader's decision is not solely his to make. In part, Vader is carried to that decision by life itself. Vader was born Anakin Skywalker, a slave on a remote world, who by chance met Jedi Master Qui-Gon Jinn. Qui-Gon began Anakin's Jedi training, an education that put him in a position to be tempted by the dark side and later, in the wake of the Clone Wars, led him to become Darth Vader. But something else happened when he met Qui-Gon; he fell in love with a girl named Padmé. He married Padmé, and they had two children, Luke and Leia. Years later it is Luke whose insight and compassion help awaken Anakin. And when he realizes the truth of things, Anakin acts for the good of others. He seizes Emperor Palpatine and saves his son's life.

Through Anakin's experience we can see that life is a vast web of cause and effect, conditioning all aspects of the universe. When we look at where we are right now we cannot say we got here all by ourselves. Whether in a prison or a penthouse, our upbringing, our education, even our nationality, all helped create our present location, status, personality, and state of mind. We cannot stand outside the network of cause and effect that is life. Rather, we are part of and conditioned by the perpetual movement of life.

Without the Emperor and his entire Sith legacy there would have been no threat to the Republic. There would have been no trade embargo of Naboo, no crisis in the Senate, no secession movement, no Clone Wars, and no destruction of the Jedi Order. Without the trade embargo of Naboo it is unlikely Anakin Skywalker would have ever found his way to the Jedi Temple, met Palpatine, and turned to the dark side. Had he never turned to the dark side he would not have battled his son. His son, in fact, would have never been born had he not met Padmé. And their meeting was contingent on the trade embargo of Naboo. Anakin needed the trade embargo, needed the Clone Wars, and needed his son to put him in the position to save the galaxy. Had conditions not come together in such a way for Anakin he may never have destroyed the Emperor in *Return of the Jedi*.

Seen from this perspective, Vader's act of killing the Emperor began long before Luke was born. It began before Anakin was born and even before Palpatine was born. Each of their lives and actions played a crucial role in setting up Anakin's heroic act, but they were all *conditioned by* their interaction with the world—and here *conditioned by* means nothing more than "influencing and becoming part of." All actions, all thoughts are conditioned by what has come before them and what is occurring simultaneously with them. I have described this as cause and effect—but that is not entirely accurate.

"Cause and effect" suggests a beginning and an end, with one thing clearly the cause and another clearly the effect, but the movement of life is continuous, without start and stop. The phrase *cause and effect* is also inadequate to describe life's intricate nexus of conditionality because it indicates only a single chain of events. Life, however, is not a two-dimensional line; it is multi-dimensional and conditioned from all directions. Everything has an impact on everything else. Consequently, life is, in a sense, guided by the interaction of conditions. Yet this gives only a partial, and overmechanized, picture of life, for there is another factor we need to consider: human will and action.

LET US RECALL Luke's first training session aboard the *Millennium Falcon* in *A New Hope*. Obi-Wan instructs Luke, "Remember, a Jedi can feel the Force flowing through him."

"You mean it controls your actions?" Luke asks.

"Partially, but it also obeys your commands."

We know from looking at Darth Vader's experience with the Emperor that life conditions us. When Obi-Wan says the Force "partially" controls our actions, it is like saying *life* conditions us. We are, of course, active participants in our lives. We are conditioned by the universe, but conversely, we condition it. Ideas, beliefs, salient issues flow through us from our friends, neighbors, world events, and the media. They become part of us, alter our thoughts and our actions, but we also add a bit of ourselves to them. Thoughts, feelings, and world opinion are both collective and individual. The collective contributes to our individual thoughts, feelings, and opinions; our individual thoughts, feelings, and opinions help make up the collective. The collective influences the individual, and the individual influences the collective. The two *interpenetrate* one another.

While life partially controls or conditions our actions, it is also influenced or "commanded" by those same actions; the Force obeys our commands. Luke's destiny in the original Star Wars Trilogy appeared to have only two possible conclusions. Either he would do as Obi-Wan and Yoda had instructed him to do and destroy his father, or he would turn to the dark side. Everything in his life propels him to this fork in the road. Yet when he reaches it he chooses neither. Instead he casts his lightsaber aside; he does not kill, and he does not fall to the dark side. He makes a choice that was not controlled by destiny.

With all this talk of interdependence, interpenetration, emptiness, and conditionality we may be tempted to conclude that our existence itself is just an illusion. That is not so. We are really here. It would be no "illusion" if you were punched in the nose, it would be painful!

RECALL THE THEED RAINBOW from chapter IV. We saw

that it exists because of the interplay of air, water vapor, sunlight, and our perspective and perception. All those factors (and many others) come together, and through their interplay there is a rainbow. But beyond these factors there is no thing that we can say *is by itself* the rainbow. Like the rainbow, we too are formations. The five aggregates come together, and through their interplay there is this thing we call the human being. There is no unchanging, separate, independent "self" that *is by itself* a human being— nonetheless human beings do exist. We are neither an illusion nor permanent and distinct.

We live in a deeply interconnected relationship with all of life. That interconnection means you affect me and I affect you. Moreover, that interconnection means I affect *me*. The fact of impermanence reveals that we are never the same person from one moment to the next. Because of this, my thoughts and actions of today affect the "me" of tomorrow. Life partially controls who I am, but it also is conditioned by my will and my actions. Our willful acts and thoughts do matter—they can make the world a better place (for example, Vader's decision to save his son), or they can make the world a hell (Vader's decision to turn to the dark side). It is our volitional acts, our will, that in Buddhism are called *karma.*

Karma is an intentional action or thought. It is the action or thought itself, and not the *result* of an intentional action or thought, as is sometimes believed. Reading this book is karma; the result one acquires from reading this book is called "karmic fruit"—the result of the seeds of karma coming to fruition. For there to be karmic fruit there must be intentional action or thought.

Karmic fruit—or the "effect" in the cause-and-effect relationship—is an extension of the lesson of conditionality. Who we are tomorrow is conditioned by our willed acts today. "Good" karma—action that leads to freedom from suffering—yields "good" karmic fruit. "Bad" karma—action that leads to more suffering—yields "bad" karmic fruit. If our actions are "good" today it is more likely we will experience happiness tomorrow. If they are "bad," suffering will result.

The Buddha put it this way, "The doer of evil reaps suffering, here and hereafter, in both states remembering, 'I have committed evil.' Not only here, but hereafter, he experiences more suffering because he has gone to a state of suffering. The doer of good deeds reaps happiness, here and hereafter, in both states remembering, 'I have done good deeds.' And there is more joy, because he has gone to a blissful state." (It's important to be clear that one needn't believe in "future lives" to understand the word *hereafter* in this passage—as we will see more clearly below, *hereafter* can simply refer to the moments, days, and years yet to come in your life.)

Karma is not a cosmic decree of justice or system of reward and punishment. If you break your leg today it is not because you swore at your brother yesterday. That is not the functioning of the law of karma. The remorse you feel for swearing at your brother is the fruit of karma, not the fact of the bone fracture. Similarly, an act of kindness does not necessarily always produce happiness—the *intention* behind the action or thought is of critical importance. If one performs a kind deed in the hope of being rewarded by the stars or God than that deed is not "good" karma.

IN "A NEW HOPE" Han Solo helps rescue Princess Leia from the Death Star. He also helps deliver Artoo Detoo—the bearer of the vital Death Star plans—to the Rebel Alliance. On the surface Han's actions were "good" karma, but his intentions were another matter entirely. He tells Leia he had no interest in her or her revolution but expected to be well paid for his help. He was in it for the money.

The intention behind Han's heroism was *greed*. Greed is not itself "bad" because some authority says so, or because of some moral decree in some doctrine. Greed is "bad" because it is based on a wrong view of the self. Greed is founded in discrimination and separation between you and me, in other words, ignorance—the shroud of the dark side. We know the shroud of the dark side is a source of suffering, and because greed is founded in ignorance, suffering is the natural result of it or any other "bad" karma.

Thinking can be "good" or "bad" as well. Planning to kill your father is "bad" karma. Thinking about murdering your father for a second but then dismissing the thought is "good" karma. When we anguish over a "bad" action or thought from our past we may be experiencing karmic fruit of the regret variety. Regret itself can be "good" or "bad." Dwelling on our regret and treating ourselves callously for our unskillful past can create a guilt complex that will perpetuate the stream of "bad" karma in our life. However, regret that is investigated with Yoda's method of calm reflection can offer insight that leads to "good" karmic results. Han's apparent regret for abandoning the rebels to fight the Death Star alone was of the latter type.

Remember the closing scenes of *A New Hope*. Suspense builds as Luke Skywalker, pursued by Imperial agents, races his X-wing down a Death Star trench toward his target—a small thermal exhaust port right below the main port. If he fires true he will destroy the most destructive weapon ever created. If he fails the rebellion is doomed and the Empire's reign of terror will continue unabated. There is nothing that separates him from the three enemy TIE-fighters behind him. Their leader, Darth Vader, gets Luke's ship in his sites and prepares to fire the killing shot. Just at that moment laser fire strikes one of Vader's wingmen, destroying the fighter. The remaining wingman panics, bumps into Vader's ship, and sends it reeling into space. Luke looks around wondering who fired the saving blasts. Over his intercom he hears Han's triumphant yell followed by, "You're all clear, kid. Now let's blow this thing and go home!"

Han expresses regret over abandoning Luke and the rebels to fight the Death Star alone when he responds to Chewbacca's reproachful growl with, "What're you looking at? I know what I'm doing." However, Han is sensitive and thoughtful enough to recognize that his greed has produced suffering. And so instead of wallowing in guilt and deepening his suffering, Han is wise enough to let go of his selfish desire and greed, and acts for the benefit of others.

YODA TELLS LUKE in *The Empire Strikes Back,* "If once you

start down the dark path, forever will it dominate your destiny, consume you it will, as it did Obi-Wan's apprentice." The teaching of karma demonstrates that our actions today stay with us and impact us tomorrow. Obi-Wan's apprentice, Anakin Skywalker, becomes Darth Vader—in that action he makes certain his journey down the dark path, and once he starts it consumes him, dominating future actions. Vader becomes trapped by the dark side; every evil act he commits takes him deeper into the dark side and makes it harder and harder for him to break the karmic chain of his malefactions until evil seemed his only choice.

If we take Yoda's words above as absolute truth we may think that, like Vader seems to be, we too are dominated by our choices and actions, that they entirely consume us, but recall the following from *Return of the Jedi.*

"You cannot escape your destiny," Obi-Wan tells Luke. "You must face Darth Vader again."

"I can't kill my own father," Luke says, almost pleading.

"Then the Emperor has already won."

Later, as Luke stands over his fallen father prepared to destroy him the Emperor is ecstatic. He gleefully says, "Good! Your hate has made you powerful. Now, fulfill your destiny and take your father's place at my side!"

By this point Luke is a Jedi, a Jedi that sees through the shroud of the dark side and perceives life with right view. To kill Vader, as Obi-Wan wants, will place Luke exactly where the Emperor desires him—at the Sith Lord's side. Either choice will produce the same result: the dark side. But Luke is not controlled by destiny. He is free to choose, and his choice saves the galaxy.

While our present state of mind is in large part based on our past karma, we must not adhere to a doctrine of determinism and believe that everything that happens is simply fate or that our past actions enmesh us into a specific pattern of behavior from which we can never escape. Yoda claims Vader's destiny is forever dominated by the dark side, but we know that is not true. There is no doubt that Vader's karma leads to the dark side and keeps him there for decades, but his will allows him to choose a different path, a path of compassion. That new choice saves his son and frees Anakin from the dark-side prison he had constructed. Our karma can set us down paths that consume us, but those paths need not "forever dominate our destiny." We have will, and we can choose our actions for good or ill. If we pay attention to the teaching of karma, we see that it actually emphasizes rather than ignores the importance of human will. And despite its often-mentioned "destiny," the Star Wars saga as a whole portrays agreement with this view.

KARMA IS NOT A DIFFICULT TEACHING to understand. In

fact, it is commonsensical and even occurs in other religions as well. Jesus expressed the fact of karma with his expression, "As you sow, so shall you reap." If you sow seeds of jealousy, greed, and hatred you will reap the sorrow of them. If you sow seeds of kindness, compassion, and love you will reap the joy they bring. Moreover, greed is itself an unpleasant state of mind. Kindness, in contrast, is a pleasant state of mind.

The teaching on karma becomes more complicated, however, when we realize that karmic fruit can ripen not just in this lifetime, but in the next. But what does this really mean? On the one hand we have emptiness: The human being is empty, made up of five aggregates each of which are themselves empty and constantly changing. There is no permanent, separate self and no soul. On the other hand there is rebirth. It is important to see rebirth as moment-to-moment and forever. Each moment of life is a birth and a death. Joy arises in us and fades away. Perceptions come and go. A skin cell dies and another is reborn. Therefore, despite the fact we have no permanent or separate self we have lived through countless deaths since we first picked up this book. Every moment we are born, and every moment we die, and through it all we continue. Death—the final destruction of our main reactor—is no different.

This, or course, is hard to swallow. When someone we know dies they are not just different from what they were a moment ago, they are gone. They don't come out and have a mock lightsaber duel with us when we knock on their door. But, remember the rainbow: a variety of conditions formed it. One of those conditions is sunlight. So, what happens to the rainbow when the sun sets and night falls? Does it die? Does it become nothing?

The truth is the rainbow has not become nothing just because we don't see it; it has simply changed. The water vapor that helped give it life has now floated up to form a cloud. The air that held the vapor has moved with the changes in atmospheric pressure created by nightfall to become wind rushing through the hair of

Jamillia, the Queen of Naboo—in fact becoming part of her as she breathes it.

The rainbow is no longer there for us to enjoy as a rainbow, and our friend who passed is longer there for us to enjoy hitting upside the head with the cardboard tubing we pretend is actually Vader's saber. But neither our friend nor the rainbow has become nothing. If we look deeply we will see them again.

Just as the person you are at this moment is an extension of the person you were in the previous moment, the shape you take after the body shuts down is a continuation of who you were at the instant of death. That means our will, desire, craving, feelings, perceptions, and so forth carry on. But what does that mean?

One Buddhist monk puts it this way: "As there is no permanent, unchanging substance, nothing [like a self of soul] passes from one moment to the next. So quite obviously, nothing permanent or unchanging can pass or transmigrate from one life to the next. It is a series that continues unbroken, but changes every moment."

The Buddha used a very simple model to reconcile the insight of no self and rebirth. He took a lit candle and indicated that the flame represented a human being. Then taking another candle he touched the unlit wick against the flame of the first candle. The wick caught fire and there was a flame on the second candle. The flame on the second candle is a continuation of the flame on the first. We cannot say that the second flame *is* the first because they are clearly on two different candles. At the same time, however, we cannot say that they are wholly different because one directly gave rise to the other. We can take five, ten, a hundred candles and light one off the other. The flame on each would be an extension of the one before it. None the same and none different.

"Similarly," continues the monk quoted above, "a person who

dies here and [a person who is born] elsewhere is neither the same person, nor another. It is the continuity of the same series. The difference between death and birth is only a thought-moment: the last thought-moment of this life conditions the first thought-moment of the so-called next life."

So the question "What exactly is reborn?" is not a proper question. *Nothing* is reborn—but everything continues. Life is movement. Life is continuation. We can experience karmic fruit from a "past life" because we are a continuation of that life. Birth and death are merely ideas—nothing separates us from one moment to the next. Think about this and evaluate its truth for yourself.

Seeing life as continuity, not being caught in the ideas of birth and death is itself freedom, and this freedom, called *nirvana,* is the subject of our next chapter.

VIII NIRVANA

AND THE WAY OF THE FORCE

*"The Force is…an energy field created by all living things.
It surrounds us and penetrates us. It binds the galaxy together."*

OBI-WAN KENOBI
IN "A NEW HOPE"

*"You must feel the Force around you.
Here, between you…me…the tree…the rock…everywhere!"*

MASTER YODA
IN "THE EMPIRE STRIKES BACK"

MOMENTS BEFORE YODA DIES, he shows wisdom when he says his death is "the way of things…the way of the Force." The way of things, of life, is *emptiness;* notions of birth and death, self and other are misleading and the cause of suffering. The extinction of these notions transcends suffering, and this transcendence is called *nirvana*.

Nirvana is a difficult topic to address largely due to the numerous misconceptions of it floating around our halls of education and taverns of conversation. Many believe nirvana is a sort of blissed-out mental trance that one enters to rise above the world. Others imagine nirvana as distinct from our daily life. Some consider it to be *beyond* this life, almost like Heaven, or the moons of Iego, where Anakin claims angels come from. Another common error is the notion that nirvana is something one "attains," perhaps after sitting cross-legged at the top of the Jedi Temple for years.

Some of the confusion over what nirvana exactly is can be traced to the diversity of its definitions. Nirvana has been described as "the getting rid of craving," "the stopping of becoming," "calming of all conditioned things," "detachment," that which is "devoid of desire and passion," "stopping, renunciation, surrender, release, lack of clinging," "freedom," and many, many other things.

This wide range of characterization is not due to any vacillation on the part of the Buddha, who first used the term. Nor is it the result of disagreement among Buddhist masters. Rather, it is caused by the very nature of nirvana itself. The difficulty with defining nirvana is that it is beyond all concepts and ideas.

Because human language is dependent on conceptualization for communication the nature of nirvana makes accurately expressing it impossible. Nirvana is the very absence of ideas and conceptualization. It is beyond notions of "good" and "bad," "birth" and "death," and "happy" and "sad." It cannot be classified as "this" in relation to "that." This is because nirvana is what *IS*. It is reality in its purest form free from ideas and classifications.

Because nirvana is inexpressible many Buddhists have attempted to convey its meaning without the use of concepts. In the Zen tradition, monks are provided with *koans* such as "What is the sound of one hand clapping?" or "Who were you three hundred years before your parents were born?" or "If a tree fell on the Wookiee homeworld of Kashyyyk and no one was there to hear it, would it make a sound?" These enigmas are not meant to be logically deduced. In fact they *cannot* be. The koan is a way of using words to take a person beyond them by jarring the mind out of its usual rut. Koans help the monk free his mind from conceptualization and open it to the pure emptiness of nirvana.

Efforts to express nirvana without language of notions or ideas originated from one of the Buddha's most famous teachings, the Flower Sermon. It was here that the Buddha most eloquently expressed nirvana by simply holding up a lotus flower. He said not a word, just stood, lotus in hand. Just this. There is no clearer way to express nirvana.

Although any conceptual communication of nirvana is wholly insufficient to fully comprehend it, we are left with little choice but to use the tool of language if we wish to proceed. *Nirvana* literally means "extinction." In the time of the Buddha a common metaphor for suffering was the burning of fire. The Buddha remarked "All is burning"—including our eyes, body, and mind—

with the fire of suffering. When this fire is put out, extinguished, nirvana is revealed.

The fire of suffering is extinguished when identification with and attachment to desire and composite phenomena is put to an end. We've seen that for a fire to burn certain conditions are necessary. Those conditions are heat, fuel, and oxygen. If one of those conditions is removed the fire is removed. Our suffering is like a blazing fire—it burns because of specific karmic conditions. Among those conditions is attachment. If attachment is removed the fire of suffering is extinguished. The Eightfold Path (which we will talk more about in the next chapter) outlines the way that helps us calm impulses, wrong views, and other things that result in our attachment or aversion to aspects of life. Similarly, we can say Yoda's "way of the Force" is the practice of calm reflection, mindfulness, and deep commitment that transcends the dark side path. With calmness and mindfulness—supported by understanding of what Yoda calls "the way of things"—the fire of suffering goes out.

Although this path helps us extinguish the fire of suffering it does not produce nirvana. If the removal of one condition (such as the condition of suffering) produced nirvana then it would be subject to the influence of other conditions. Such a thing could not offer total freedom from suffering because it would be impermanent and bound to the interplay of cause and effect. In other words, the freedom it offered would be temporary and incomplete. Nirvana, however, is not bound to conditions. That is why it cannot be produced. Nirvana simply *IS*.

When we say nirvana "*IS*" we mean that it is everything and everywhere. It is within us, around us, on us, in the air, the sea, and the toilet. It is in the Emperor's greed, Padmé's love, Jabba's villainy, and Luke's compassion. At the same time it is none of these things because it is beyond all notions of duality and relativity. Nirvana is unchanging and undying, it transcends birth and death, past, present, and future. It is the pervasive ground of all being.

BY REFLECTING ON THE FORCE we can learn more

about nirvana. Let us recall what Obi-Wan and Yoda said of it in the original trilogy. In *A New Hope,* Obi-Wan Kenobi describes the Force as an energy field created by all living things. "It surrounds us," he says, "and penetrates us. It binds the galaxy together." Yoda echoes Obi-Wan in *The Empire Strikes Back:* "Life creates [the Force], makes it grow. Its energy surrounds us and binds us....You must feel the Force around you. Here, between you...me...the tree...the rock...everywhere!"

We may mistakenly imagine the Force as some sort of invisible river of magical energy or an intangible well of mystical power that can be accessed and manipulated. This perception sets up the Force as distinct from us, a tool used by a Jedi or Sith to compel others or to batter foes. But if we listen deeply to what Obi-Wan and Yoda say we see that the Force, like nirvana, is not separate from us, it is a part of us—surrounding, penetrating, and binding us with it and the galaxy.

The Force, Obi-Wan tell us, surrounds us. Everywhere we look the Force is present. That means when Luke battles TIE-fighters in the darkness of space the Force is there. When he flounders through the snowdrifts of Hoth he is with the Force. Yoda says the Force is here and everywhere. No matter where Yoda, Luke, or even Han Solo find themselves—the Force is there. The same is true with nirvana. It is everywhere, within us and around us in this very moment.

The Jedi say the Force binds the galaxy together. We can imagine this is like saying all things in the galaxy are interdependent. The air depends on the tree and the tree depends on the air. The two are bound up with each other. This sort of relationship we have been calling interdependence, but it could just as easily be called the Force or nirvana. The reality is that the two—air and tree—are inseparable. However we describe these things, the label does not alter the reality.

Obi-Wan says the Force surrounds us and binds us, and it also penetrates us. It enters into our body from every direction. Penetrating us it becomes part of us. We know from Qui-Gon Jinn that the Force is present in every living cell in the form of midichlorians. The midichlorians are the source of all life. Qui-Gon told Anakin Skywalker in *The Phantom Menace,* "Without the midichlorians life could not exist." In turn, Yoda revealed to Luke the fact that life creates the Force. Put simply, the Force produces the life of midichlorians and this life creates the Force. The Force creates life and life creates the Force. This cycle is present in every living cell, in everything—a relationship of interpenetration.

SOME SPEAK OF BECOMING "ONE WITH" the Force or "entering" into nirvana. Such ideas are misleading. A person cannot *become* something he already is. Based on our interpretation of the Force we know that Luke was already one with the Force long before he began his Jedi training. Luke cannot exist outside of the

Force because it penetrates him and he in turn penetrates it. In fact, he and the Force exist in perpetual interpenetration. Likewise, nirvana is not something entered into. Nirvana is not found outside or later—we *are* nirvana, right here, right now. Looking deeply we see that there is absolutely no distinction between Luke and the Force, nor any between nirvana and us.

Our nature is the nature of nirvana. It is part of us like a Tatooine sand dune is part of Tatooine or a Kamino wave is part of the ocean. The wave may seem to be distinct from the ocean, but both wave and ocean are by nature water. In the same way, we are merely waves of nirvana forming, breaking, and returning to the source. We arise from nirvana, we live our lives as nirvana, and we return to nirvana having never left it. We are a *formation* of nirvana—of all that is. Just as the wave's nature is water our nature is nirvana. Therefore it is incorrect to think of a person entering nirvana or attaining it. A wave cannot "attain" water because it *is* water.

We labor under the illusion that we are our mind and body and our life is limited. This is a false belief that brings us a great deal of suffering. We suffer because, like the Emperor, we fear death. We are afraid of death because our understanding is shrouded by the dark side and that gives us an incorrect idea of what death is. When we don't see with Obi-Wan's deep perception of emptiness we believe we are bound to our bodies, our perceptions, our ideas. We are conceived and born; we mature, decay, and die. This is our lifespan, and we believe that from something we become nothing.

The word *nirvana* means extinction—but not just the extinction of suffering; it is also the extinction of dualistic thinking. In chapter IV we learned that the rock Luke had lifted with the Force and his submerged X-wing were different only in Luke's mind.

Nirvana is the destroyer of dualistic thinking, of concepts, of ideas, and of all barriers. Nirvana destroys the ideas of self and other, one and many, birth and death, existence and nonexistence. Investigating life with mindfulness and effort we can also destroy these barriers that exist only in the mind. Looking deeply we can see that we are part of all of life. Our bodies, thoughts, and consciousness are not distinct from the world; they do not exist independently—our true nature is the nature of the undying nirvana.

Death does not reduce us to nothing. We can never become nothing because our nature is emptiness and that means we are made up of everything. The practice of living Force mindfulness allows us to touch our no birth, no death nature and helps us remove the shroud of the dark side and see the truth that life just IS, and we can never be outside it. This realization shatters the illusion of death.

Within the human being is the world, the arising of the world, the cessation of the world, and the path leading to the cessation of the world. The entire world exists within each of us. This is the insight of emptiness, of Obi-Wan's symbiont circle. At this moment we are one with all things, we are one with the Force. Suffering, the arising of suffering, nirvana, and the path reveling nirvana are not outside of us; they are in every cell of our body.

When we follow the Buddha's way of practice, detailed by the Noble Eightfold Path, nirvana is revealed to us. When a Jedi has the deepest commitment and the most serious mind she practices Qui-Gon's mindfulness of the living Force and Yoda's calm, passive reflection and "the way of the Force" is revealed. The Buddha's way does not produce nirvana; it merely helps us remove the shroud of the dark side, the veil of ignorance, so we can recognize it. A person who can live every moment with equanimity, in constant mindfulness of life, of the living Force, watching the rise and fall of phenomena with detachment, unswayed by craving, is truly free and beyond the grasp of the dark side of suffering. Such a person is not fooled by form; she cannot fall victim to the false belief that she is her body. She does not cling to the five aggregates of self as though they were permanent. She cannot look upon the evil Darth Vader and fail to see the goodness present in him. She is not attached to concepts and ideas, but dwells in the midst of life and accepts "the way of things."

Yet, again, this does not mean she no longer feels anger or sorrow. Feelings continue to rise and fall according to the usual flow of life. The difference is she is no longer bound by her feelings like Anakin was in *Attack of the Clones*. Feelings arise, and she is mindful of their arising. Feelings touch her and fade away. Because she claims nothing as hers, she can watch her emotions with detachment, and they touch her very lightly, and they cannot drive her into disastrous acts of slaughter.

Happiness is said to be a *mark of nirvana*. Shariputra, a leading disciple of the Buddha, said that nirvana was the greatest happiness. It is a happiness that one cannot describe because it is happiness of non-attachment, happiness beyond word or description. We cannot comprehend this happiness unless we *experience* it, but it is understood to be a happiness much more profound than our daily delights. For example, the happiness we feel from getting a great seat to the first midnight showing of *The Phantom Menace* is subject to the vicissitudes of life—that is, we become disappointed because the movie is not what we hoped it would be (although Darth Maul *is* pretty cool!). Nirvana, however, is happiness free from the need for things to be a certain way, to be different from how they are. Since it is free of unnecessary desire it is not subject to the ebb and flow of life. It is happiness that is complete and unblemished. It is happiness that is untroubled and pervasive.

Many of the definitions of nirvana are expressed in "negative" terms. In the above paragraph "free of unnecessary desire" is used to describe the happiness of nirvana. There are other examples, such as "getting rid of craving," "renunciation," and "lack of cling-ing." These imply a division between nirvana and other things (e.g., craving). As we have seen, however, nirvana is everything, so nothing can stand outside it or against it. The use of these "neg-ative" terms is not meant to demonstrate nirvana in relation to "non-nirvana," but to show us what needs to be absent from our mind for us to fully perceive nirvana.

While "negative" terms seem to exclude, nirvana itself does not. It is not heaven as opposed to hell, good side as opposed to dark. Nirvana is beyond all such concepts. That means it is heaven and at the same time it is hell.

EXAMINE THE FORCE with the insight of interdependence and interpenetration. On the surface, it may appear that the Force is divided. There is the good side of the Jedi and the dark side of the Sith. But from our deep looking, we see that the two cannot exist independently; they need each other. The good side is defined by the dark, and vice versa. Without the dark side there would be no frame of reference for the good side. Good would have no definition, no meaning without evil. So, the instant there is something that can be called "good" there must be something that can be called "evil." As with everything else, good is by nature empty of a separate self. Therefore, looking deeply into the good side of the Force we find the dark side.* In Buddhist terms you cannot have nirvana without *samsara*. Samsara is the suffering in life. It is the perpetual cycle of craving, attainment, loss, and sorrow that we are bound up in.

Yoda tells Luke in *The Empire Strikes Back*, "If once you start down the dark path, forever will it dominate your destiny." Although we have the free will to make our destiny, once we start chasing after craving and clinging to false ideas we are already walking the dark path. If we don't learn to stop ourselves and let go of unwholesome ways of living, the cycle of samsara will continue to dominate our destiny.

It is common to think that nirvana and samsara are opposites. One is the cessation of suffering, and the other is bondage to suffering. However, like the dual aspects of the Force, nirvana and samsara interpenetrate one another. Nirvana is itself the ground of being, and thus it is the totality of everything else, including samsara. Look for the truth of this in your own life.

The lesson we learn from understanding the nature of nirvana can free us from the dark path of samsara. A person seeking to release himself from his suffering, if he is wise, will not reject his suffering. He need not escape samsara to discover nirvana. Nirvana is already present in samsara. It is through embracing his suffering that he discovers transcendence from it. It is by accepting life as it is in its gains and losses, its joyful times and its sorrowful

---

*Although good and evil cannot be pinned down with absolute moral permanency, this does not mean we should live our lives willy-nilly, hedonistically pursuing each of our selfish desires, without causing problems for ourselves and others. Each of our actions has an effect on the world. Each of our actions matter. Our actions can cause suffering or bring joy. Please chose your actions carefully.

times, that he resides in a place of peace and freedom. This is the ultimate truth of nirvana. It is the truth of nonduality.

The difference between nirvana and samsara, the good side and the dark side, is nothing more than a thought. Nirvana and samsara are not separate realities but *reality itself* seen with different states of mind. The dualistic mind sees reality as samsara. The awakened mind sees nirvana. To turn our world of samsara into nirvana we need only change our mind.

The Buddha said, "Observing life deeply, it is possible to clearly see all that is. Not enslaved by anything, it is possible to put aside all craving, resulting in a life of peace and joy."

Observing life deeply, we are not bound to the path of the dark side; we do not walk down it to be forever dominated by samsara. But when we have lost our way, we may "give in to our anger," and then, as the insidious Emperor says, "our journey to the dark side will be complete." In the next chapter we will examine the Eightfold Path, the way that keeps us from being consumed by the shadows of the dark side.

IX THE EIGHTFOLD PATH

THAT TRANSCENDS THE DARK SIDE

"Your focus determines your reality."

JEDI MASTER QUI-GON JINN
IN "THE PHANTOM MENACE"

LUKE is repeatedly warned to beware the dark side. If Luke is not aware of the dark side as it arises within him, he might become swept away by it and suffer his father's fate. The Eightfold Path is the way that helps us refrain from doing things that lead us to the dark side, that cause us to suffer.

The Buddha was the creator and original master of the Eightfold Path. "Wherever the Eightfold Path is practiced," the Buddha taught, "joy, peace, and insight are there." Thus the Eightfold Path does not lead us away from the dark side *to* nirvana, but when practiced correctly, the Path *is* nirvana. In other words, the Path is not a means to an end like the Jedi trials. The Path is a reward in itself. To walk the Path is to walk in happiness.

The eight factors of the Path are grouped into the three categories of Moral Virtue, Meditative Cultivation, and Wisdom. The perfection of these three aspects of the human being is essential for nirvana to be realized. In the first category, Moral Virtue, is right speech, right action, and right livelihood.

RIGHT SPEECH

In *The Phantom Menace*, Padmé uses *right speech* when she reminds Anakin that his anger is only natural and that it is not his fault that his mother died. Not only were these words true, they were also kind and loving. Right speech requires the use of truthful, loving words intended to inspire self-confidence, joy, and hope in others.

Implicit in this definition is abstention from telling lies, from gossip and discordant words, and from abusive or cruel language.

Chancellor Palpatine, the master of the dark side, was also a master of violating right speech. In *Attack of the Clones,* after years of careful manipulation and deception, Palpatine has finally obtained what he sought—emergency powers to rule the Republic like a tyrant. His first words upon receiving this authority are the darkest of lies. With mock sincerity he says, "It is with great reluctance that I have agreed to this calling. I love democracy—I love the Republic. The power you give me I will lay down when this crisis has abated." Of course he never intended to relinquish his authority and, instead, goes on to rule through terror and murder for decades.

Violation of right speech is not a "sin" in the sense used by Judaism and Christianity. Violating right speech, telling lies and using words that create division, is not an act one is punished for at some time in the future. The wage of lying is suffering. "All beings are the owners of their deeds, the heirs of their deeds; their deeds are the womb from which they spring. Whatever deeds they do—good or evil—of such they will be the heirs." This is true with all the factors of moral virtue: speech, action, and livelihood.

Palpatine's deeds, his lies and deception, do not wait until some imagined afterlife to produce suffering. They bring him suffering in the midst of his rule as Emperor. He can find no joy in the authority he achieved through guile and so he sits in the dark, a shriveled figure, scheming and suffering.

One final note on right speech is worth our time. Along with avoiding speech of dissension and falsehood it is suggested that one abstain from vain and idle talk. With right speech, words are viewed as a treasure that should only be brought out when they are useful and when the time is right.

The meaningless babble of Jar Jar Binks and the incessant complaining of See-Threepio, for example, fail to meet this criterion. Right speech, in this case, means we learn when to listen deeply and not talk. By listening deeply to others, as Padmé listened to Anakin, we can hear what they are saying and what is being left unsaid. This affords us the opportunity to find the "right" thing to say, the loving and supportive words that lessen the burdens of others.

RIGHT ACTION

One way to investigate our actions is to look at their results, the fruit they produce. If it is sour and distasteful like some slimy meal of Jabba the Hutt, if it is the fruit of suffering, then the action is not right action. If the fruit is sweet and brings us and others true joy like the tasty Naboo fruit Anakin and Padmé enjoyed, then it is likely that the action is right action. Being mindful of the living force and our bodily actions will allow us to recognize the variety of fruit they produce. But it is important that we are careful not to believe our actions are right just because we experience some trivial pleasure. Eating food that is delicious but harmful to our body is not right action. Having sex with many partners may be invigorating, but it does not promote true peace and happiness. In fact it can create a lot of loneliness and pain.

Right action, the second element of the category of Moral Virtue, is concerned with action of the body. In *The Empire Strikes Back* Yoda reminds us that "anger, fear, aggression" are dark side energies that can overwhelm us and start us "down the dark path." When we are on the dark path our actions can cause pain and suffering. It is important that we use Yoda's method of calm reflection to investigate our actions and see if they bring peace and happiness to others and ourselves.

To practice right action earnestly it is essential that we investigate the intentions behind our actions. Generosity is right action when it is the act of giving without any expectation of return. Anakin's offer to help the stranded Qui-Gon Jinn and Padmé in *The Phantom Menace* is an example of right action. Giving ourselves in time and material resources to those in need is a true act of compassion and one that is a joy unto itself. But if the intention behind the act is not grounded in compassion, then it can lead to the dark side.

RIGHT LIVELIHOOD

The final factor of the moral virtue is right livelihood. One way to see if we are practicing right livelihood is to compare our trade with that of Jabba the Hutt. Jabba has his fat, stubby fingers in many of the pots that led to the dark side. He dealt largely in illegal "spice" trade—an illicit drug in the Star Wars galaxy. He also transacts business in the slave trade. He has many slaves himself, and some he fed to the Rancor, a creature he kept caged and tormented in his dungeon. Jabba uses deception and violence to maintain his position.

If we look at any job and find that Jabba has a strong presence there we may want to reflect on the direction of that employment and see if it is leading to happiness or suffering. To walk the Way that transcends the dark side it is essential that we find means of employment that support our intention to cultivate wisdom and compassion in our heart and mind. Vocations that contribute to suffering in us and in others are not "right."

RIGHT EFFORT

The second category of the Path is the category of Meditative Cultivation. Meditative Cultivation focuses on nurturing heart and mind through right effort, right mindfulness, and right concentration. Right effort was discussed in chapter VI as the Jedi practice of deep commitment and serious mind. We saw that right effort was diligent action or thought that led to spiritual freedom.

There are four functions to right effort. The first is to return unwholesome seeds that have blossomed in our mind consciousness to our storehouse consciousness. "Unwholesome" means anything that does not correlate with peace, happiness, and freedom. This means, among other things, the dark side energies of fear, anger, and aggression. The Emperor tempts Luke to the dark side in *Return of the Jedi*: "Use your aggressive feelings, boy! Let the hate flow through you."

When hate and aggressive, dark side feelings have entered our consciousness we can remember to practice as Qui-Gon taught and become aware of the present moment and the state of our mind. Recognizing the presence of the dark side in us, we do not allow it to pull us into actions that we will regret. We practice mindful breathing and allow the emotion to pass, and in this way we stay off the path of suffering.

Letting go of dark side energies is complemented by the second function of right effort: preventing unwholesome seeds from manifesting in the mind. Although hatred, anger, aggression and other mental formations of the dark side are unwholesome, if we are practicing the way that transcends the dark side, they can nonetheless be transformed into wholesome elements. If we recognize the dark side when it is present in our mind we can practice Yoda's method of calm reflection and gain insight into our hate and aggression and the things that have helped them arise.

In *The Empire Strikes Back* Princess Leia is upset at Han Solo for suggesting she has romantic feelings for him: "Why, you stuck-up…half-witted…scruffy-looking…*nerf-herder!*" And, of course, we remember Han's wonderfully conceited retort: "Who's scruffy-looking?" But it was what he says next that is insightful: "I must have hit her pretty close to the mark to get her all riled up like that…."

If Leia had reflected on her anger toward Han, and her frigid-ness toward him earlier in the film, she may have recognized that she does indeed have feelings for him, feelings that her pride would not allow her to face. Understanding the root of her anger may have helped her not be hostile toward Han and allowed her to treat him with more kindness (no matter how much he played the scoundrel). Therefore, understanding the causes of our unwholesome behavior can help us keep from running headlong down the path of the dark side.

The third function of right effort is to bring wholesome seeds up from the storehouse consciousness into the mind conscious-ness. Wholesome seeds are not ideas about living a chaste, upright life. Rather, they are those things that bring us peace, joy, and free-dom on a deeply spiritual level. Living simply, taking time to enjoy life, and to appreciate our loved ones are ways one can practice the third function.

Once wholesome seeds have bloomed in our mind conscious-ness we can turn to the final function of right effort, namely keep-ing them there. We can keep wholesome seeds strong in our mind by nourishing them with mindfulness and concentration. Breathing in and out in mindfulness is an ever present light of peace that brings ease and contentment.

RIGHT MINDFULNESS AND RIGHT CONCENTRATION

Right mindfulness and right concentration are the other two aspects of Meditative Contemplation. Throughout this book we have seen how important mindfulness and concentration are to the Jedi and to every Buddhist practice. The most important of those practices is meditation, which will be explored in detail in chapter XI.

RIGHT VIEW

The final category of the Eightfold Path, the Way that transcends the dark side, is Wisdom. Wisdom is the aspect of ourselves that is developed through profound investigation into life. The two parts of Wisdom are *right view* and *right thought*.

Right view is the understanding of things as they truly are that gives rise to a mind free from the shroud of the dark side. We have discussed right view at great length in other chapters (see pages 43–45, for example). Right view should change the way we look upon the world, as divided and separate, so we see it as it truly is—interdependent and interpenetrated, unified through Obi-Wan's symbiont circle.

RIGHT THOUGHT

In *The Phantom Menace* Qui-Gon tells young Anakin Skywalker, "Always remember, your focus determines your reality."

The second factor of wisdom is right thought. Thought is the forerunner of all action. What we think initiates what we do and say. The focus of our thoughts directs our deeds. If one's thoughts are kind and serene, right action will follow—and so will happiness—as surely and as closely as one's shadow.

Right thought is thought that releases dark side energies when they arise in the mind and channels the mind in the direction of the good side of the Force, the place where loving kindness and compassion are dominant. Right thought is the fostering of selflessness and love for all beings in our mind.

In *The Phantom Menace* Obi-Wan Kenobi refers to Jar Jar Binks and Anakin Skywalker as "pathetic life-forms" because they continually get in the way of what Obi-Wan thinks is the best thing to do. This is not right thought. Thinking of other people or things as obstacles in our life creates division and conflict. Right thought does not exclude. It is inclusive—concerned for the well-being of all life-forms.

This does not mean we have to *like* everyone we come in contact with. But if we are trapped in the idea that they are nothing more than a bother or a representation of what we find contemptible then we are not recognizing their true nature. It is important to keep our hearts open and observe people and phenomena deeply before we pass judgment. We must reflect as Yoda has instructed and ask ourselves, *Am I sure this person is the way I think he is? Am I attached to views and wrong perceptions that are making me narrow-minded and unable to see the truth about this person? Are my opinions rooted in fear and insecurity or prejudice and ignorance?* These types of questions help us to be mindful and to pass beyond the shroud of the dark side.

THE JEDI DO NOT RELY ON OTHERS to hone their

skills with the Force. Nor do they just *theorize* about the power
they wield through the Force. Jedi have the deepest commitment
to their training, and they develop their mindfulness in every
moment. We can learn from the Jedi and commit ourselves to the
Eightfold Path this very moment.

The Eightfold Path, which is also called the Dharma path, is the
way of freedom, the way that trascends the dark side. It brings liberation from worry, fear, doubt, confusion, and insecurity. It offers
us the opportunity to let go of selfish, petty desires and to embrace
love for all beings. It provides us with methods to calm our mind
and to understand suffering. But to experience the benefits of the
Eightfold Path it is up to us as individuals to practice it.

And when we do practice it, we see it develops wisdom and
compassion, the two great qualities of the human being, and the
very energies, as we will see in the next chapter, perfected by Luke
Skywalker.

X LUKE SKYWALKER'S

PRACTICE OF WISDOM

"You were once Anakin Skywalker, my father."

"That name no longer has any meaning for me."

"It is the name of your true self. You've only forgotten.
I know there is good in you.
The Emperor hasn't driven it from you fully....
Search your feelings, Father....I feel the conflict within you.
Let go of your hate."

LUKE SKYWALKER AND DARTH VADER
IN "RETURN OF THE JEDI"

THE DHARMA PATH, in some ways like the way of the Jedi, is the path of understanding and love. When the Path is walked the two great qualities of humankind are developed: wisdom (also called understanding) and compassion (also called love).

Wisdom is the result of careful observation of our nature and the nature of life. Wisdom is the fruit of meditative contemplation (like Yoda's calm reflection), mindfulness (as Qui-Gon taught), and diligent effort (like the deep commitment and serious mind of a Jedi). Wisdom is the insight of the way things are that frees us from the ignorance of the dark side. Compassion is unconditional love. It is the love that has no expectations and draws no distinction between friend and enemy. Compassion does not withhold its love, and the gifts it offers contain no strings. Like the twin suns of Tatooine, wisdom and compassion give light and life to the world of darkness.

Unless wisdom and compassion are cultivated equally problems can arise. Compassion developed without wisdom can produce a kind-hearted fool like Jar Jar Binks; while a strong mind developed without compassion can produce a heartless manipulator like Jabba the Hutt.

IN STAR WARS it is Luke Skywalker in the saga's final chapter that best exemplifies wisdom and compassion. In *Return of the Jedi* Luke has developed these qualities of being better than any Jedi before him—even better than his Master Obi-Wan.

Luke's true Jedi mastery is demonstrated by the fact that he allows himself to be vulnerable to suffering. By doing so he discovers an inner strength greater than that of any Jedi of his time and even of the previous era of the Jedi's ascendancy. After his confrontation with Darth Vader in *The Empire Strikes Back,* Luke knows good still remains in his father. Obi-Wan, however, cannot see this. He is attached to the view that Vader is "more machine than man, twisted and evil." Obi-Wan fails to look deeply, to see past the vile acts of Vader and recognize the heart of a man who was suffering terribly. Luke does not make the same mistake. He saw that his father had forgotten himself and needed to be offered understanding and compassion in order to be retuned to the good side.

In *Return of the Jedi* Luke's wisdom and compassion propel him to turn himself over to the Empire in order to rescue his father. He tells Leia, "There is good in him, I felt it. He won't turn me over to the Emperor. I can save him. I can turn him back to the good side. I have to try." Luke allows himself to be made a prisoner of the Empire in order to "save" Vader, to draw his father out of suffering. Offering understanding and compassion, Luke appeals to the good Anakin that remained in the shadows of Darth Vader. Reminding him of his life before he turned to evil Luke says, "You were once Anakin Skywalker, my father." "That name," Vader replies, "no longer has any meaning for me."

"It is the name of your true self," Luke says. "You've only forgotten. I know there is good in you. The Emperor hasn't driven it from you fully." Then Luke directs his father back to himself, to look deeply into his own nature: "Search your feelings, Father.... I feel the conflict within you. Let go of your hate"—for it is Vader's *attachment* to hatred, hatred for himself, for his crimes, among other things, that perpetuates his suffering.

It's important we see in this that even Luke Skywalker, with his great mastery of the Jedi ways, of understanding and compassion, cannot with his own power "turn" Vader away from the path of the dark side. This is always the case. We can only offer others compassionate support and wise advice, but only they themselves can remove the shroud of ignorance from their heart and mind. Luke does not tell Vader what he *should* or *should not* do, he simply directs Vader back to himself, to search his own feelings, to investigate his own mind and discover the truth that it is not "too late" for him, that he can still lift himself out of the dark side. This is the Jedi way, and it is also the Dharma way.

IN FAIRNESS TO OBI-WAN, he may have been aware that

his friend and pupil, Anakin Skywalker, was suffering miserably. In *Revenge of the Sith* we see how Obi-Wan "once thought" as Luke does and how he tries to draw Anakin out of the dark side. But when Anakin feels betrayed and flies into anger, Obi-Wan senses his friend is lost to the dark side and shuts his heart to his onetime Padawan.

When someone hurts us, as Anakin hurt Obi-Wan, Padmé, and so many others, the natural tendency is to want to punish him or push him away so as to protect ourselves and others from further hurt. That could be why Obi-Wan insisted Luke kill his father—to make Vader suffer for the pain he caused Obi-Wan and others. But Obi-Wan's desire to punish Vader and to exclude him from his heart are themselves forms of suffering. Obi-Wan suffers as much as Anakin does.

True compassion, true love never produces suffering. It is not granted only to those who satisfy our desires. It is not reserved for the happy and prosperous. It is given to everyone, and without conditions. Luke is able to have compassion for his father because he has the wisdom to recognize the *source* of his father's evil. That source was not Vader himself, but Vader's ignorance, attachments, misperceptions, self-hate, and his inability to see a way off his karmic path of the dark side.

THERE IS NO MORE COMPASSIONATE ACT one person can do for another than offer oneself in order to free another from misery. But even Luke's profound understanding and love falters in the bowels of the Death Star:

Time and time again Luke tries to escape from dueling Vader. He shuts off his lightsaber, he retreats from Vader's attack, and he even hides in order to avoid conflict. However, when Vader threatens Luke's sister, Leia, the young Jedi's composure weakens and in a fury he assaults his father.

Luke beats Vader back with his lightsaber, driving him to the ground. Then, with a vicious strike, he cuts his father's hand off above the wrist. Just as Luke was prepared to deliver the death-blow he heard the Emperor's sinister cackle. "Good!" cries the elated Sith Master, "Your hate has made you powerful. Now, fulfill your destiny and take your father's place at my side!"

In this moment, Luke sees that, just like his father, he has become ensnared by hate. Looking at Vader's mechanical stump of an arm, then at his own mechanical, black-gloved hand, Luke realizes he has indeed become like his father. If Luke kills Vader he will not destroy the evil of Anakin Skywalker, but only replace it with a new evil—the evil of Luke Skywalker. The failures of Anakin, the weakness of that poor man, are part of Luke as well. Luke understands the truth that the evil in his father is also in him. It was an evil grounded in misguided intentions, mistaken betrayal, ignorance, fear, and self-hate. Realizing this removes Darth Vader's sinister appearance and reveals a sad, pitiable man—a man trapped by his own suffering. Looking down at his prone father, compassion swells in Luke's heart, and he switches off his lightsaber.

"Never!" he says tossing his weapon aside. "I'll never turn to the dark side."

Luke at this moment does what his father could not do, he transcends suffering. His wisdom parts the shroud of ignorance and shows him that the dark side cannot give him power to "rule the galaxy" or to "save his friends," it can only lead to the misery his father suffered. Accepting this he is able to let go of his hate saying, "I'll never turn to the dark side." Armed now with only wisdom and compassion he does something no weapon can ever do—he defeats the hate in his heart.

LUKE'S ACTIONS show us that ultimately the good side of the Force is stronger than the dark side. The good side is stronger because it *includes* the dark side. Without suffering there can be no wisdom. When we suffer well, that is, when we mindfully investigate our suffering, we learn from it. *Suffering is a good thing.*

Let me repeat that: the dark side, suffering, is a good thing. It is good because it gives us something to work with, something to investigate. Looking deeply into our suffering is how we understand life, how we develop wisdom. And this is necessary to transcend the dark side. With wisdom comes compassion because when we recognize the way things truly are and understand why we suffer we can't help but to love all beings and to help them release their mechanical grip of the dark side.

Yet be very clear: to say suffering or the dark side is a good thing does not mean that we should ever "give in to hate," but that we should recognize it when it is present in us and investigate it, learn from it, understand. This is how we bring balance to our lives.

In the Star Wars saga, balance is brought to the Force when Vader defeats the Emperor and removes the plague of the dark side from the galaxy. But the true balance, inner balance, comes earlier: when Vader learns from Luke's wisdom and compassion and mindfully embraces the suffering within himself, understands it, and releases its causes. Anakin may have told Luke that he "saved" him, but it is Anakin's own choice to finally face the dark side within him with courage and honesty that frees him from it and opens his heart to compassion. To be in the grips of suffering is to be out of balance, but the practice of recognizing and investigating pain brings harmony to the Force and reveals the presence of nirvana.

WHILE LUKE SKYWALKER best exemplifies the qualities
of wisdom and compassion in Star Wars, it is his father, Anakin,
who shows us the full range of what it is to be human. Anakin goes
from a sweet kid to an arrogant, temperamental young man, to a
monster cloaked in the dark side. In his life, he loved people, at
times he hated himself, he sought the approval of his teachers, he
selflessly tried to help others, he made mistakes, and he inten-
tionally committed crimes of ignorance and of wickedness. But in
the end he finds freedom from the dark side.

Many of us think we are not worthy of freedom and love
because we believe we are bad. We note our failings, weaknesses,
prejudices, and all the ugly qualities about ourselves and think,
"I am no good, I am a liar, a fake. I mistreat people and think
cruel thoughts of my friends and loved ones. I am a loser and a
failure in everything I do." We think the way of wisdom and
compassion and the practice of mindfulness are beyond us
because there is so much hatred, anger, and fear in our heart, and
because we find it so difficult to remain in the present moment.
We have become so trapped in the darkness of our own suffering
and delusion that we fail to see the light of peace, joy, and freedom available to us right now.

Yet the lesson of Anakin's experience teaches us that everyone,
even the most wicked, has the seed of liberation in his heart. That
seed is waiting for us to help it grow. We can help it grow right
now by learning to *stop*. We stop being controlled by the poison-
ous stream of negative thinking that judges us and demands perfection. We stop succumbing to our own self-loathing and
self-pity and come back to our true selves and to the truth that we
are not these terrible things we think we are—we are not solely

our "sins" and errors. We stop and allow ourselves to release the idea that we are unworthy. We are worthy. Each of us is worthy of love, compassion, and understanding. Each of us is capable of letting go of the self-hatred and unhappiness in our heart.

If Darth Vader can find freedom then each of us can too!

XI TRANSFORMING

OUR JAR JAR NATURE

"Meditate on this, I will."

MASTER YODA
IN "ATTACK OF THE CLONES"

THE JEDI PRACTICE MEDITATION.

Luke's training under Yoda on Dagobah is a form of meditative concentration—albeit one practiced while upside-down! Qui-Gon observes and calms his fears and aggressive feelings with meditation. Anakin meditates on the growing dread and anxiety he feels over his mother's plight. And Yoda meditates to investigate the dark side and the mysteries of life.

Despite a common misconception, meditation is not meant to cut us off from the world or to avoid life. Meditation is a practice that helps us experience life fully—to get in touch with reality as it truly is. If a Jedi were to meditate in the way taught by the Buddha he would be confronting life directly, he would not run from himself or find things to distract him. He would sit, breathe, and observe his mind with equanimity and compassion. And from this process the freedom that is understanding develops.

Meditation is the practice of focusing the mind so we become aware of its conditions in the present moment. We observe feelings, thoughts, memories, and desires as impermanent. Even the idea of self—the belief "I am this little green body" or "I am a Jedi Master"—is recognized as transitory. We observe feelings and thoughts, but we do not grasp them, and so they fade away. In time meditation brings us to understand, not just intellectually but in our heart, that whatever is of the nature to arise is of the nature to cease. Deep understanding of this frees us from attachment to desperate thoughts like, "I must marry her," or "I must destroy the Jedi Order."

Luke enters the dark side cave on Dagobah in order to confront himself, to face his suffering. This is precisely what meditation is. It is the conscious act of calmly taking a look around the depths of our own mind. There are a lot of frightening and ugly things in there, a lot of dark-side elements, but we are careful not to attach to them. We recognize and examine them, calmly, as Yoda instructs Luke to do. We do not reject or ignore them. We discover that they are complexes, fears, desires, and misunderstandings that are both deep and shallow. But by observing them we realize they are all impermanent, and we slowly remove layer after layer of the dark side shroud.

It is important to develop understanding of the impermanent nature of things. One way to do this is by observing our feelings. Feelings can be pleasant, neutral, or unpleasant. A pleasant feeling could be the excitement and anticipation we feel when the words "A long time ago in a galaxy far, far away…" appear on the screen. A neutral feeling could be sleepiness on the third night of camping out for the midnight showing of *Revenge of the Sith*. An unpleasant feeling could be listening to Jar Jar Binks talk.

Pleasant feelings arise in one context, and unpleasant manifest in another. External phenomena and our perceptions of them have an impact on the sensations and thoughts we experience. As phenomena and perceptions shift, feelings alter as well. Observing our feelings we discover that they are not solely "ours." Feelings are formations that are produced by a variety of components. Misperceptions, habits, biology, the food we eat, and objects of perception all impact the way we feel. With meditation we realize that the feeling we experience is just *a* feeling and not *my* feeling. This practice helps cultivate equanimity in us—a quality highly regarded among the Jedi!

IN "THE PHANTOM MENACE," as Obi-Wan Kenobi hangs desperately just below the rim of the Theed melting pit, he could have easily been lost in his despair. His master lies dying a few feet away, and with Darth Maul poised to strike, his own life seems finished as well. But Obi-Wan steadies himself. Breathing calmly he lets his fear and worry float past him, he remains composed in the face of incredible strain—and he defeats Darth Maul. Later he is confirmed a Jedi Knight for his actions and, presumably, for his display of equanimity.

Equanimity means remaining centered in the midst of life regardless of the intensity of the experience. When a pleasant or unpleasant feeling arises we notice it. We may appreciate a pleasant feeling, but our appreciation should not go so far as to become attachment. Attachment to a pleasant feeling produces suffering when that feeling leaves us. Calmly letting go of a pleasant feeling as it fades is being equanimous. The same is true with unpleasant feelings like anger and hatred. As anger and hatred manifest in us we can use Obi-Wan as a model and follow our breath, remaining centered so our emotions do not carry us away.

Powerful feelings—like anger and hatred—can overwhelm us as they do Anakin at the Tusken camp. That is why Yoda and Obi-Wan Kenobi warn Luke in *The Empire Strikes Back* to beware of anger and not to give in to hate. Those feelings lead to the dark side.

Meditating on our feelings helps us better understand ourselves. Contemplating the mind and the activities of the mind can also deepen self-awareness. In meditation we observe the thoughts, desires, and moods of the mind. Sometimes it is as calm as still water, and other times it is as raucous as the crowd at the Boonta Eve race. But outside of meditation, when our mindfulness is weak, the mind typically functions like Jar Jar Binks. Jar Jar's attention is noticeably unfocused on what he is doing. He fumbles with a tool and gets shocked in the process, his thoughts drift away from his bodily movements and he steps in something foul, he is mesmerized by his visual appetite and confuses conversation. Jar Jar's unmindfulness causes him and others (and us too when we see him on screen!) a great deal of grief. His unmindfulness leads to banishment from his home, ostracizes him from others, and—on several occasions—nearly gets him killed.

OUR MINDS TOO HAVE "JAR JAR NATURE."

When Jar Jar nature is in full possession of us we do things unskillfully and we bring discomfort to ourselves and to others. We can "transform the Jar Jar within" by practicing mindful breathing, bringing our awareness to the present, scattered state of our mind. Awareness of Jar Jar nature does not mean we try to make our mind shut up or lock it away in some room like Obi-Wan does to the real Jar Jar in *The Phantom Menace* (well, the CG one, at least). We just observe our hyperactive mind and allow it to be that way for as long as it needs to be. If we continue to breath mindfully, without self-judgment or expectation, the Jar Jar within will calm down (but it's natural if this takes a long, long time—so don't get discouraged). Sometimes, when the mind is particularly overrun by our galactically restless Gungan nature, we might find it difficult to keep our attention on the breath. That is why it is sometimes good to move our attention away from the head, away from our thinking, and focus it down in the abdomen. We take our mindful breathing low, noticing the rise and fall of the abdomen with each breath.

We can learn from the Jedi in this. Dueling the Dark Lord of the Sith, Darth Maul, in *The Phantom Menace*, Qui-Gon Jinn finds himself in a narrow corridor. His mind is focused on destroying Maul when suddenly the corridor's laser gates slam shut separating him from his opponent. Sensing his opportunity to end the Sith Lord momentarily gone, the Jedi master does not become distracted by lost opportunities nor does he grow anxious about the future. Qui-Gon drops low to his knees, shuts his eyes, and focuses his attention on his breath. Qui-Gon does not flee the moment; he does not attempt to mentally escape the grim peril across from him; he merely takes his breathing low, observing his mind and body.

Qui-Gon's practice helps us keep from being swept away by our thinking, our worrying, and our anxiety. If we are caught up in our thinking we cannot be in direct contact with life. As Qui-Gon tells Anakin, "Remember, concentrate on the moment. Feel, don't think." Of course, we don't just *shut out* our thoughts, but with mindfulness we become aware of them, watch them, and this means we are no longer outright controlled by them.

We have seen Qui-Gon's method of meditation. Now let's look more closely at the mechanics of meditation so we can practice it too.

TO MEDITATE, FIND A POSITION IN WHICH YOU

can comfortably hold your back erect. Keeping the back straight prevents you from drifting off to sleep if you become drowsy (as often happens when we first begin to practice meditation), and it also helps reduce strain on your shoulders and lower back. It also allows you to breathe naturally. Aside from holding the back erect, the rest of the position does not matter much. You can sit cross-legged like Master Yoda,* in a kneeling posture as preferred by Master Qui-Gon Jinn, or even, in imitation of Anakin Skywalker, standing. If you prefer a chair (and don't worry that Darth Vader seemed to like this position too!), that is an equally fine option as well. The point, in the beginning, is to be able to sit comfortably for some time until you get used to the practice.

As you sit in meditation you can bring your attention to your body. You may notice that your jaw is clenched or your shoulders are tense. We carry a lot of stress in those areas of the body. So we scan our body from the top of our bald, wrinkly head, down to our pointy, green ears and all they way to our bare, clawed feet, relaxing any muscles that are tensed.

With the inhalation, know you are breathing in. With the exhalation, know you are breathing out. Do this by focusing on the natural process of breathing. Do not try to induce a trance or escape into another state of consciousness—just breathe and observe mind and body. There is no place you need to go, no star system or Jedi status that you can attain that could be better or

---

*If you choose to sit in what is known as the lotus position or half-lotus position be sure to use a cushion to sit on and have your knees firmly on the ground, not lifted up off it.

offer more of life than what is here in this moment—so just be aware of it.

If during meditation you find that your thoughts are no longer on your breath but reliving past lightsaber duels or trying to unravel the mystery of Anakin's origins, you will want to diligently—and without judging yourself harshly!—bring your attention back to your breath. Do not become angry if your mind has drifted off to a galaxy far, far away—just return your awareness to the breath. Meditation is not a challenge to be overcome; it is a gift to be enjoyed—the gift of the present moment.

In the beginning you may find it difficult to keep your mind in contact with the rhythm of your breath. That is natural—your own "Jar Jar nature"—that fidgety, erratic, spastic quality—is the nature of our mind, and it does not want to pay attention to something so boring as our breath. So we may want to look for ways to help keep our attention from bouncing off the walls and, instead, directed on our breath.

One helpful technique is silently counting our breaths. For each cycle of inhalation and exhalation count one. *In...out,* "one." *In...out,* "two." *In...out,* "three." All the way to ten, and then back down to one again. It doesn't matter if you get to ten—it doesn't even matter if you get to three! If you lose count or your mind drifts away, just resume counting from one. Do not become discouraged if it is difficult to remain focused. Mindfulness is a part of each and every one of us; the more we practice, the stronger our mindfulness will become—it just takes time and Jedi-style commitment.

BESIDES SITTING MEDITATION THERE IS ANOTHER

type of meditative practice that we can employ: walking meditation. Walking meditation uses the same principles as sitting meditation just with the added dimension of movement. We don't see Jedi practicing walking meditation in the Star Wars saga, but we can imagine them strolling carefully and mindfully through the Jedi Temple and along starship corridors. There is a nobility to their walk and a grace that suggests a calm, even mind.

Walking meditation is a very good way for us to practice unifying mind, breath, and bodily action. It begins with taking one step as you breath in and another step as you breath out. Your steps are the same as always. You do not exaggerate the movement or walk stiffly. You simply walk as you usually do, but now you are able to enjoy and appreciate your steps in mindfulness. You can do this practice anywhere, at anytime. However, when you are in the markets of Mos Espa, attending a session of the Galactic Senate or running late for a class with Master Yoda you may want to increase the pace of your walk. You may take three or four steps for each inhalation and exhalation. The number of steps depends on your own individual rhythm—I imagine Master Even Piell takes more steps in a breath than a larger Jedi like Master Yarael Poof. It does not matter whether you take two or six steps, or whether you stand 1.2 meters or 2.6, just as long as you remain mindful of your walking.

MEDITATION HELPS US reflect on the world and ourselves calmly and passively as Yoda teaches Luke to do. It helps us see the world as it is without the shroud of the dark side clouding our vision. It allows us to investigate the dark side within us and see that all things arise due to specific causes, and then fade away when those causes are absent.

SECTION II:
THE PADAWAN HANDBOOK

THE PADAWAN HANDBOOK:

ZEN CONTEMPLATIONS FOR THE WOULD-BE JEDI

Contemplations on Worthy Conduct

O APPRENTICE,
the way of mindfulness is a difficult one. Commit
yourself completely. Always remain diligent because
the path of practice is narrow and continuously assailed
by the energies of the dark side.

WHO IS BETTER PROTECTED:
a Jedi with a legion of his fellow Knights at his side,
surrounded by a squadron of Battle Tanks and Ground
Assault Vehicles or one who conducts himself with honesty
and kindness, whose behavior is upright, and whose
thoughts are lovingly directed toward all beings? Clearly,
one who conducts himself with honesty and kindness,
whose behavior is upright, and whose thoughts are
lovingly directed toward all beings is better protected
because he has guarded himself against the internal
armies of the dark side that assail his mind.

APPRENTICE, IT IS BEST NOT TO SPEAK,
to tell others how they should live,
let your life be your teaching.

SELF-PRIDE IS A COMPLEX THAT EATS THE HEART
and mind of all, including the Jedi. If you think you are
greater than other beings, equal to other beings, or less
than other beings you have succumbed to self-pride. Guard
against these three complexes night and day.

THE GREATEST OF ALL JEDI

is not the one who defeats a thousand opponents; he is the one who triumphs over himself. Without patience one cannot truly call himself a student of the Way. Develop your patience—make impulse and whim as common to you as honesty and morality are to a Hutt.

DO NOT ABANDON THOSE WHO ARE SUFFERING.

Do not close your eyes to those in pain. Commit yourself to finding ways to be with those who are gripped by the dark side, so that you can understand their situation deeply and help relieve them of their anguish.

BE AN INSPIRATION TO YOUR FELLOW BEINGS.

Carry yourself with grace and kindness. Do not allow arrogance to distinguish you like fools in martial attire, draped with emblems and medals. A Jedi should wear the simple cloak of his order with humility. When those who avoid the Way, pursuing only what is pleasant, attached to the senses, see one conducted so, they will experience their loss and lament their ways.

YOUNG PUPIL ALWAYS REMEMBER:

Where there is anger, offer kindness.

Where there is selfishness, offer generosity.

Where there is despair, offer hope.

Where there are lies, offer truth.

Where there is injury, offer forgiveness.

Where there is sorrow, offer joy.

Where there is hatred, offer love.

Where there is evil, offer goodness.

Contemplations on Attachment and Desire

BEWARE OF THE BINDING TRACTOR-BEAM
of attachment. For a being that is attached to his body, his thoughts, his feelings, beliefs, perceptions, or consciousness is imprisoned and can never know true freedom.

TO COMMIT TO THE WAY
is to give up selfish desires and to live for the benefit of all beings, Gungans, Jedi, and Sith.

THE JOY THAT ARISES
with bodily pleasure offers fleeting benefits and little sweetness. It is fruit that quickly becomes bitter and over time poisons the one who eats it. The joy that arises with equanimity, that is free from attachment to sensual desires, is sweet and nourishing. Its benefits are profound and ever present. Look carefully, young one, at the objects you desire. Are they truly what you believe them to be? What resides in them that does not reside everywhere? What do they hold that cannot be found in every element of the galaxy?

AMBITION AND DESIRE LEAD TO THE DARK SIDE.
Be wise, my determined apprentice, there is no happiness like the happiness of having few desires.

Contemplations on Compassion

A JEDI WHO IS WORTHY KEEPS COMPASSION foremost in his thoughts. His compassion extends to all beings in the galaxy. With an open and loving heart he directs these thoughts for their universal benefit:

MAY TERRESTRIAL BEINGS, arboreal beings, beings of the skies, beings of the seas and oceans, beings of the stars and asteroids, beings visible and invisible, beings living and yet to live, may they all dwell in a state of bliss, free from injury and sorrow, tranquil and contented. May no one harm another, deceive another, oppress another, or put another in danger. May all beings love and protect each other just as a Master loves and protects his Padawan. May boundless love pervade the entire galaxy.

Contemplations on the Finitude of Life

THE EYES ARE THE TOOLS OF DECEPTION
that conjure the illusion of death. Look! See! There is no
death, young one, except that which exists in the mind
shrouded by the dark side.

REMEMBER: DEATH LURKS AROUND EVERY CORNER,
and it cannot be bargained with. Knowing this,
if you are wise, you will put aside all quarrels.

LIFE IS PRECIOUS TO ALL BEINGS.
All beings fear death. Knowing this, my young apprentice,
and caring for others as you care for yourself,
do not be eager to deal out death.

YOU CANNOT ESCAPE DEATH,
young one. Death, not just of the corporeal body,
but of all manifestations of the mind, is inevitable. It
is the way of all things, "the way of the Force."

WHEN SOMEONE IS DYING OF THIRST
it is too late to dig a well. If you wait until you are upon
your deathbed to practice the Way it will be too late. Death
will not wait a moment longer than it is ready. Do not be
lazy, O Learner, be steadfast as a serious,
deeply committed Jedi is steadfast.

LIFE IS IMPERMANENCE.

All things are subject to change, and nothing can last for-ever. Look at your hand, young one, and ask yourself, "Whose hand is this?" Can your hand correctly be called "yours"? Or is it the hand of your mother, the hand of your father. Reflect on the impermanent nature of your hand, the hand that you once sucked in your mother's womb.

Contemplations on the Dark Side

A JEDI WHO IS RULED BY ANGER,
by hatred, by jealousy, by desire is bound to the dark side just as a swoop is bound to terrestrial flight.

A JEDI WHO HARBORS RESENTMENT
and holds on to the thought, "He was cruel to me and showed me no respect," nourishes the dark side energy of hatred in himself. A Jedi who lets go of resentment and releases his damaged ego uproots hatred from himself.

IGNORANCE IS THE PATH TO THE DARK SIDE.
One who is practicing the Way must always keep his mind open. He must observe, listen, and learn. The Truth is found in the most unlikely of places.

LIKE BIKER-SCOUTS AT THE HEAD OF AN ARMY,
thought is the vanguard of all action. If your thoughts are influenced by the dark side, your actions will be evil. Observe your thoughts carefully, for they may be leading you down the path of the dark side.

ANGER IS A POWERFUL EMOTION OF THE DARK SIDE.
It can destroy harmony and lead to argument, conflict,
and even death. When anger arises in you do not give
in to it. Remain mindful, observing the anger, but not
acting upon it. If you believe someone else is the cause
of your anger, look at that person compassionately—they
may be trapped in the dark side.

HATRED CANNOT DEFEAT HATRED, O APPRENTICE.
If hatred is directed toward you combat it with kindness.
That is the only way to defeat hatred.

Contemplations
on Wise Action

BEFORE YOU ACT, YOUNG ONE, YOU MUST REFLECT.
Reflect unwisely and troubles follow as surely as a droid
follows the mandates of his programming. Reflect wisely
and troubles are like a shadow in the void of space,
unseen and unfelt.

WHEN ACTING ALWAYS ASK YOURSELF,
"Does this action support my true happiness and the true
happiness of others? Does this action support my aspiration
to transform the energies of the dark side within me?" If you
can answer, "yes" to both these questions then
you may be sure your action is worthy of the Way.

THOUGHTS ARE LIKE TRACTOR-BEAMS
that pull you off course. When you act, act!
There is no room for thought.

O APPRENTICE,
you inherit the results of your actions in body, speech, and
mind. The ground you stand on today was produced by
your actions of yesterday. Actions of worthy conduct
produce a stable foundation. Unworthy actions produce
a path strewn with boulders and pitfalls.

Contemplations
on the Mind

CONTROL THE MIND.

Hold it like a cup of water in the hand—still and calm.

IF YOU ARE NOT AWARE OF YOUR MIND,

young one, you cannot know it. If you do not know your
mind, you cannot care for it. If do not care for your mind,
you cannot nourish it and grow in wisdom.

O LEARNER, YOU MUST TAME THE MIND

like a handler tames a reek. As an untamed reek can
bite and gore so too can the untamed mind arouse
thoughts of ignorance, selfish desire, and delusion that
bite and gore the spirit.

THE BLADE OF A LIGHTSABER IS ONLY AS GOOD

as its adegan crystal. If the crystal is impure, poorly cut, and
fractured, the blade will be dangerous and poor. If, on the
other hand, the crystal is pure, well cut, and not fractured,
the blade is safe and good. The same is true with the mind.
If the mind is impure, poorly trained, and unfocused the
resultant life will be dangerous and poor. But a pure
mind, well trained and focused, will bring about a life
that is both safe and good.

O APPRENTICE,
you must recognize and abandon the impurities of
your mind, the impurities of anger, hatred, aggression,
fear, despair, avarice, superfluous desire, obstinacy,
arrogance, and jealousy. When you are able to
abandon the afflictions of the mind
you will find serenity and happiness.

Contemplations on Mindfulness

WHETHER SITTING, STANDING, WALKING,
or lying down, be mindful day and night of your
bodily position and actions. Whether pleasant, neutral,
or unpleasant, be mindful day and night of your feelings.
Whether kind, impartial, or cruel, be mindful day and
night of your thoughts. Whether focused, ambivalent,
or dispersed be mindful day and night of your
state of mind.

DWELLING IN MEDITATION,
the mind is at peace—emotions rise like a hungry
Gooba fish; left alone they cannot disturb the surface.

HARMONY ARISES WHEN THERE IS BALANCE.
Balance arises when there is equanimity. Equanimity is the
fruit of mindfulness and patience. Take your time, young
one, perform every action with complete awareness, and
harmony will be your reward.

ATTENTION TO THE MOMENT
reveals what is hidden. With mindfulness of the "living
Force" it is possible to know what is unknown.

MINDFULNESS IS THE WAY OF OBSERVING
that the past no longer exists and the future has not yet
arrived. It is the way of dwelling peacefully in the
present moment, free from both desire and aversion.
To live in mindfulness is to be free of anxieties,
regrets, desires, and fears.

FOCUS ON WHAT YOU ARE DOING.
Concentration should be fully directed on the object of
your inquiry, the object of your task, like the beam
of an ion cannon is focused on its target.

Contemplations
on Time

ALWAYS IN MOTION THE FUTURE IS
because it is unborn, unsubstantial. It is merely an image,
like a hologram of a living being. We can no more touch
and feel the future than we can touch and feel a hologram.
The future, then, is unreal because it is not present.
Only the present is real; only this moment is alive.

WHEN CONSIDERING THE PAST OR THE FUTURE,
dear Apprentice, be mindful of the present. If, while considering the past, you become caught in the past, lost in the
past, or enslaved by the past, then you have forgotten yourself in the present. If, while considering the future, you
become caught in the future, lost in the future, or enslaved
by the future, then you have forgotten yourself in the present.
Conversely, when considering the past, if you do not
become caught, lost, or enslaved by the past, then you
have remained mindful of the present. And if, when considering the future, you do not become caught, lost, or
enslaved in the future, then you have remained
mindful of the present.

Contemplations on Wisdom

THE TRUE WEAPON IS THE LIGHTSABER OF WISDOM,
which cuts the bonds of ignorance from our mind.

A JEDI OUGHT TO CHOOSE HIS WORDS CAREFULLY
and intelligently. A single word of wisdom says more
than a thousand words spoken idly. Thoroughly listen
and reflect. The words you utter can have a profound
impact on the listener. Will they bring peace
or will they cause harm?

WISDOM EXISTS
when you understand something and recognize
that you understand it, and when you do not
understand something and you recognize that
you do not understand it.
That is wisdom.

LIKE THE TWIN SUNS OF TATOOINE,
wisdom and compassion give light and life
to the world of darkness.

O APPRENTICE,
do not cling to views or bind yourself to ideology.
The knowledge you now have is not changeless,
absolute truth. Truth is found in the observation of life
and is continuously learned and relearned. Be open
to the experiences and insights of others; do not
remain fixed to a single point of view.

RELEASE ALL HOLDS ON DOCTRINE OR DOGMA,
even Jedi ones, and you will be
counted among the wise.

AFTERWORD:

THE JEDI
AND
VIOLENCE

AS A PERSON LOOKING AT STAR WARS from a Buddhist perspective, I would be remiss were I not to address the issue of violence in those movies. The Buddha's teachings are explicitly nonviolent. Killing and maiming very clearly, in the Buddhist view, leads to suffering. Those acts produce suffering in the one killed or injured, in her family and friends, and in the attacker. Acts of violence can be motivated by anger, hatred, ambition, and jealousy—all factors of the dark side. But can they ever be motivated by compassion? The traditional Buddhist answer is an unequivocal "No," and I don't recommend anyone pursue any path of violence—yet I think there is something important to be learned about ourselves and the nature of violence by looking at the way violence is used by the Jedi Knights.

Can we accept the wise and venerable Jedi, the so-called "guardians of peace and justice," as beings of understanding and love when they use their powers to destroy others caught in the web of ignorance and suffering? If their acts of violence are committed out of anger, hatred, or aggression can we say the Jedi have transcended the dark side, that they act from a place of compassion? Let us analyze some specific moments from the Star Wars series.

We will start with *The Phantom Menace*. In this episode, Darth Maul kills Qui-Gon Jinn out of hatred and ambition: hatred for all things Jedi and ambition to help his master rule the galaxy. Qui-Gon Jinn's murder may have sparked hatred in the heart of Obi-Wan

Kenobi causing the Jedi apprentice to follow in the footsteps of the Sith apprentice. Obi-Wan's scream, "Nooooo!" for example, seems more enraged than anguished, as his face contorts into what may described as determined rage. It is the energy of that rage that he apparently used to engage Darth Maul in a furious battle of lightsabers. Maul was acting out of hatred, and Obi-Wan retaliated with what also may have been hatred. If this is true, if the young Jedi is motivated by anger, aggression, or hatred, then there is very little difference between the "evil" Darth Maul and the "good" Obi-Wan Kenobi. The dark side of hatred was strong in both.

Before Obi-Wan destroys Maul he has a moment to gather himself and reflect. He hangs, weaponless, above a long shaft leading to a fiery death. During this time Obi-Wan calms his mind, releasing fear, worry, and hatred, before he draws upon his powers to rise out of the clutches of death and destroy Darth Maul. The question is, When he actually killed Maul was there hatred in his heart or did those few seconds of reprieve allow him to recognize Maul's suffering and strike him down with sympathy? Did he kill out of some sort of desperate act of compassion to save his dying master? Did he kill to protect the galaxy from the destructive evil of the Sith? Personally, I believe that he did kill out of compassion—for if Obi-Wan killed out of hatred than he may as well don the black cloak and red lightsaber of his fallen foe.

We may believe that Obi-Wan cannot be like Maul even if he kills Maul out of hatred. One could argue that Obi-Wan is fighting for the good of others and Maul is after only a narrow self-interest. We may say Obi-Wan's ideals are "good" and Darth Maul's are "bad." Whether this assertion is right or wrong is not for me to say, but it is a subject worthy of our reflection.

We saw in chapter VIII that good cannot exist without evil, and vice versa. The two interpenetrate one another. To hold an idea as purely "good" is to misunderstand its true nature. There is no "good" without "evil." This is a fundamental and very important teaching. It is the teaching of emptiness, and it is something we need to continually reflect on if we hope to be free of the bonds of ignorance in our mind and release the weights of suffering from our hearts.*

Obi-Wan may have believed that because he is a Jedi he is on the "right" side, that the ideals he fought for should be achieved regardless of the means employed. He may rationalize that killing Maul is not only necessary but somehow preferable.

Similarly, in our own world, we may believe that terrorists should be destroyed at all costs, but we may fail to see the ways in which our lives, culture, and beliefs have helped create the terrorist. This is not to say that a person who commits deplorable acts of violence and murder like the perpetrators of the 9/11 attacks and their supporters should be pardoned. Of course they shouldn't! We, as compassionate humans, need to do all we can to stop terrorists, detain them, and prevent them from harming more people. But to fail to recognize our contribution—however small it might be—to the evil in the world, to say evil exists *only* in the Other, is the way we create more evil and suffering.

Simply thinking we can kill "evil-doers" and in so doing end evil is naïve. We must together confront the evil in humanity's heart, to engage people's minds with compassion and love and

---

*Again this fuzzy line between good and evil does not give us free reign to behave unkindly or selfishly. Each of our actions has consequences that can produce suffering or freedom. We must treat each action with wisdom and careful reflection.

thereby help them out of the poverty, social injustice, and the ignorance that is the cause of their dissatisfaction and hostility. We do
not need to wait until they attack to help remedy our differences.
We can act with considered goodwill now before there is more violence. This is a difficult course of action and much harder than wip-
ing them out with satellite-guided bombs or Death Star–like
weapons, but it is the only way we can stop the cycle of violence.

Love is not passive, it is active. Love is not weak, it is coura-
geous. Love means standing up to those who are harming us and
others, and stopping them. We stop them with firm hands, but
compassionate hearts. When terrorists bring violence to our shores
we must respond calmly and not allow anger or fear to overwhelm
us. We can respond with compassion in our hearts. We can
respond with fearlessness and nonviolent resolve to bring peace
and justice to the world. We can look deeply and see that commu-
nities that support violence are often acting out of fear and the
delusion that they are under attack. They may have misperceptions
about us and may see us as the terrorists. They may even say the
terrorists are right to attack us and we are wrong to attack them.

Right or wrong violence does not stop unless we set aside the
view that "they" are evil and "we" are separate from them. If we
find ways to talk with our adversaries so that we may understand
their suffering and allow them to understand ours, so that we may
make evident our "symbiotic link," we may put an end to the cycle
of violence.

Now let us turn our attention to *Attack of the Clones*. Obi-Wan
and Anakin Skywalker are in pursuit of Count Dooku, the supposed mastermind of a galactic war. Obi-Wan tells Anakin it is
important that they catch Dooku so they "can end [the] war right
now." The intention behind their thoughts of killing Dooku is

admirable. They hope to prevent an escalation of the Clone War and avert further loss of life—both acts of compassion. But their compassion does not appear to extend to Dooku himself. When they finally confront him, Anakin's anger is evident. He tells Dooku that he must pay for all the Jedi he killed that day. Thus Anakin is not motivated by compassion but by revenge.

When Anakin charges Dooku, attempting to take the Sith Lord on without the assistance of his teacher, his attack is reckless and unfocused. Anakin's mindfulness is lost to his desire to punish the fallen Jedi master. At that moment in time he is in the grips of the dark side, swept away by his anger and hatred. There is no room for understanding or compassion in him then, only the all-consuming demand for payback.

In attempting to discover whether the violent acts committed by Jedi can be described as being rooted in compassion it may be considered unwise to take the example of Anakin Skywalker. To hold him as exemplar of the Jedi is to say very little for the wisdom of that Order. After all, he did grow up to be Darth Vader. However, if we move forward along the Star Wars timeline we see that in the final chapter, *Return of the Jedi,* one of the most respected Jedi, Obi-Wan Kenobi, advocates killing without compassion.

It is in Episode VI, just after Master Yoda dies, that Obi-Wan advises Luke to destroy Darth Vader. But Luke is hesitant to take on such a task. He believes good still remains in Darth Vader, and he still hopes to help his father turn back to the good side. When he tells the deceased Jedi Knight this, Obi-Wan dismisses Luke's insight, saying Vader's humanity has been "destroyed." He informs Luke that Vader is more a twisted and evil machine than a man. Clearly Obi-Wan has very little compassion for his former pupil. He does not want to hear that there was a glimmer of kindness flickering in the blackness of the fallen Anakin. He just wants Darth Vader dead and with him the Empire and the Sith.

It is difficult for us to find a clear case of compassionate violence in the Star War series. Yet this does not necessarily mean that compassion cannot be found in violence. For the Jedi to confront violence with compassion they would need to understand first that they are not much different from their opponents. We have seen that life is interconnected. Evil does not exist outside of us. It exists in our own heart. This is the lesson Luke learned in the dark side cave on Dagobah. When we see hatred in another person we cannot truthfully say that hatred exists only in him. If we are honest and we look deeply we will see that person's hatred as a reflection of our own.

The second thing required for the Jedi to compassionately confront violence is that they recognize they are coresponsible for the evil in the world. The dark side does not spring up out of nowhere. All things are a product and a continuation of other phenomena. And all phenomena are bound together in a relationship of interpenetration and interdependence. The Sith, for example, did not appear one day from the sky. They are an offshoot of the Jedi themselves!

Over a millennia before the events of *The Phantom Menace* a group of Jedi forsook their Order to investigate the Force in a way forbidden by members of the Jedi Council. This group became known as the Dark Lords of the Sith, and they were marked as wholly evil. Shortly after the rise of the Sith, a great war took place where internecine conflict and Jedi intervention brought about the destruction of the Dark Lords. Yet, one remained. He acquired an apprentice, and over the next thousand years the secrets of the Sith were passed from master to apprentice. Century after century the Sith lived in the shadows until the time was ripe for them to reveal themselves and exact their revenge on the Jedi Order. The evil of Darth Maul and the eventual destruction of the Galactic Republic and the Jedi Knights had its beginning in the Jedi Order itself.

If the Jedi were to look deeply it would not be difficult for them to see that this "new" evil came from the heart of "good." The Sith are in fact in the Jedi, and the Jedi are in the Sith. It was Jedi dogma and strictures that stifled some Knights and contributed to their restlessness and subsequent search for greater power. This search came to fruition with the rise of the Empire and the destruction of Alderaan.

Jedi contemporary to the events of *The Phantom Menace* and *Attack of the Clones* also contributed to the rise of evil. Count Dooku, the ringleader of a group of disgruntled star systems and financial conglomerates, was a fallen Jedi. His discontent with the bloated bureaucracy of the Galactic Republic and the failures of the Senate propelled him to seek a new order to replace the decrepit old one. Many Jedi, such as Qui-Gon Jinn, are aware of the corruption in the Senate and could relate to Dooku's yearnings for a better tomorrow. When we look carefully at our enemies we will see ourselves, and we will see how our lives have contributed to their manifestation.

For the Jedi's action to be considered compassionate they must act without anger or hatred, but with the clear understanding that their opponent is caught in suffering. No matter how terrible the person may be, no matter how many deplorable deeds he has committed, it is out of delusion and pain that he acts wickedly. The evildoer is the product of his environment, negative habit energies, and his own unhappiness, confusion, and ignorance (again, this is not a justification or an excuse for wickedness, just a fact). When a Jedi sees this with a deep understanding that is free of the shroud of the dark side he will seek other means of stopping his foe that do not end with the searing death of the lightsaber. He will attack only out of necessity and with compassion for the evil-doer, whom he knows is trapped in a state of suffering. Moreover, his attack will be motivated out of love for those endangered by the Jedi's opponent.

Of course we can act without violent or murderous resolve to physically stop someone from harming others or doing evil. It can be an act of love to stop violence, and it can be done without destroying the "evildoer" or holding hatred of him in our heart. But please understand that I am in no way suggesting that this is simple; in fact it can be *very* easily twisted into righteous self-deception. For example, in our world the samurai warriors of feudal Japan believed that if their minds were "pure" they could cut off their enemies' heads and suffer no "bad" karmic consequences. This is wholly untrue. To kill with pure compassion is something very few, if any at all, can ever honestly do.

ACKNOWLEDGMENTS

My deepest gratitude extends to the Buddha, Thich Nhat Hanh, and the ancestral lineage of teachers.

Thanks to Star Wars and all its creators (who shall go unnamed for legal reasons) for the galaxy far, far away that has given me so much wonder and delight since I was as small as a Jawa, and to all the people at the major Star Wars fan sites and message boards—you've added so much to that galaxy.

I also am very grateful to all the people that contributed to the creation of this book: my insightful and expert editor Josh Bartok and the generous and kind people at Wisdom, my brother Kevin, the monks and nuns of Plum Village and Deer Park (through their wisdom and practice), the people of Clear View, Still Water Sangha, and the Wabi Sabi (especially Peggy, Chris, Larry, and Patricia), all my friends from the Teloma days to the extended Hastings family and everywhere in between, especially Sam, Chris, and Chris for their incredible friendship and crazy encouragement over the years, my parents and family for their boundless love and support (I appreciate you all more than I can say), and to the person who has been through it all with me and doesn't ever stop loving: Heather, thank you. I love you.

INDEX

ABOUT THE AUTHOR

 **MATTHEW BORTOLIN** camped out for tickets to all the Star Wars movies, and a set of Jedi robes hangs in his closet. He is an ordained member of Thich Nhat Hanh's Buddhist community, and has lived in Buddhist monasteries both in the United States and abroad. He now lives in Ventura, California.

HARDCORE ZEN
Punk Rock, Monster Movies,
and the Truth About Reality
Brad Warner
224 pages, ISBN 0-86171-380-X, $14.95

"*Hardcore Zen* isn't your typical Buddhist book. Profane and sometimes irreverent; capable of devastating, corrosive humor; Warner pulls no punches. His book is an honest account of his search for truth."
—*Booklist*

"For my money, *Hardcore Zen* is worth two or three of those Buddhism-for-Young-People books."—*Shambhala Sun*

"Gonzo; often hilarious."—*Dharmalife*

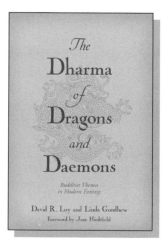

THE DHARMA OF DRAGONS AND DAEMONS
Buddhist Themes in Modern Fantasy
David R. Loy and Linda Goodhew
Foreword by Jane Hirshfield
128 pages, ISBN 0-86171-476-8, $14.95

"A veritable cottage industry now exists to examine Christian themes in popular culture, but what of the Buddhist themes? Loy and Goodhew offer a compelling foray into the dharma teachings of modern fantasy. Tolkien's *Lord of the Rings* trilogy, for example, may seem to be entirely un-Buddhist, but its preference for non-violence, shown in the repeated sparing of Gollum's life, resonates with Buddhist principles. More importantly, Frodo's quest is one of renunciation; the story is fundamentally a lesson of nonattachment. Other chapters address Michael Ende's 'Momo,' two films of Japanese anime master Hayao Miyazaki, the *Earthsea* books of Ursula Le Guin, and Philip Pullman's *His Dark Materials* trilogy."—*Publishers Weekly*

MINDFULNESS IN PLAIN ENGLISH

Revised, Expanded Edition
Bhante Gunaratana
224 pages, ISBN 0-86171-321-4, $14.95

"Extremely up-to-date and approachable, this book also serves as a very thorough FAQ for new (and not-so-new) meditators. Bhante has an engaging delivery and a straightforward voice that's hard not to like."—*Shambhala Sun*

"Of great value to newcomers...especially people without access to a teacher."
—Larry Rosenberg, author of *Breath by Breath*

ZEN MEDITATION IN PLAIN ENGLISH
John Daishin Buksbazen
Foreword by Peter Matthiessen
128 pages, ISBN 0-86171-316-8, $12.95

"Down-to-earth advice about the specifics of Zen meditation: how to position the body; how and when to breathe; what to think about. Includes helpful diagrams and even provides a checklist to help beginners remember all of the steps. A fine introduction, grounded in tradition yet adapted to contemporary life."—*Publishers Weekly*

WISDOM PUBLICATIONS

Wisdom Publications, a nonprofit publisher, is dedicated to preserving and transmitting important works from all the major Buddhist traditions as well as exploring related East-West themes.

To learn more about Wisdom, or browse our books on-line, visit our website at wisdompubs.org. You may request a copy of our mail-order catalog on-line or by writing to:

Wisdom Publications
199 Elm Street
Somerville, Massachusetts 02144 USA
Telephone: (617) 776-7416
Fax: (617) 776-7841
Email: info@wisdompubs.org
www.wisdompubs.org

THE WISDOM TRUST

As a nonprofit publisher, Wisdom is dedicated to the publication of fine Dharma books for the benefit of all sentient beings and dependent upon the kindness and generosity of sponsors in order to do so. If you would like to make a donation to Wisdom, please do so through our Somerville office. If you would like to sponsor the publication of a book, please write or email us at the address above.

Thank you.

Wisdom is a nonprofit 501(c)(3) organization affiliated with the Foundation for the Preservation of the Mahayana Tradition (FPMT).